Dedication

To my beautiful daughters, Diane & Laurie, the grands and great-grands: Joy, Dee, Michael, Jessica, John Paul III, and Justice.

Acknowledgements

Many thanks to Mr. Charles Tingley and the St. Augustine Historical Society for their help and patience. Even though they don't personally believe in ghosts, they are still very professional and willing to help with any research in the St. Augustine area. Someone told me they never had any ghosts in St. Augustine until they started the Ghost Tours. My answer was, "You had them alright, just no one ever talked about them!"

Some of the information came from articles published in the *St. Augustine Compass* by Karen Harvey. She did a tremendous job of searching out haunted areas in her town.

A lot of people were willing to talk to me about the ghosts, and a nightly ghost tour was helpful. I went on the Ghost Augustine Hearse Rides Tour one night in January, and it was cold when I was there, an icy northern wind that blew along the coast line of Florida. An enclosed vehicle seemed like the smarter thing to do. They're located at 123 St. George Street at the end of the hallway. There are numerous tours available and the people who run them are knowledgeable. The tour guide the night I was there was a man named Jonas, who has a great accent; Brian and Tom are also guides for the ghost tour company.

The pirate information was the hardest to find. There was not much in St Augustine about the pirate activity but pirates have a long history in that area.

Thanks to the ghost tour run by the Historical Museum on Third Street in Fernandina.

Thanks to TAPS—The Atlantic Paranormal Society, a good source of material about haunted places in the northeast Florida area.

I also have to include thank Doris "Dusty" Smith and her organization in Daytona Beach. She is founder of DBPRG and has numerous websites and information about the Daytona area and has written several books about her ghostly adventures. Her website address is: DBPRGinc@aol.org.

Special thanks to The Mountain Light Sanctuary, located in Asheville, North Carollina, web site: www.mtnlightsanctuary.com.

Also I would like to extend my gratitude and many thanks to some people who gave me shelter along the way:

Beverly and Jimmy Sorrells were there for me in January when I made my first trip. Thank you guys for your help and hospitality. I know Beverly is a skeptic and Jimmy just didn't say one way or the other, but they still put up with me anyway.

Another couple who have made an impact on my life and were kind to me while I was staying at their home in July and September were Dan (He died on October 30, 2007) and Audrey Champion. I was not consciously aware that when I saw Dan and Audrey in September that it would be the last time I would ever see Dan alive. On the way home I was thinking about how he did not seem to appear as well as he usually did, and it came to me then; I would never see him again. I was in Jacksonville the end of October and the first part of November to help the family with his memorial service. You will be missed dear friend. I will always remember that even in your pain, you were still making jokes about what you were going through—to try and spare others any discomfort.

And finally, I need to thank Dinah Roseberry and the people at Schiffer Publishing for their hard work and dedication. This book could not have been written without their help and guidance. Many thanks to you all.

Contents

Preface

As an original Floridian, I pretty well know my way around the First Coast area, which includes all of the northeast coast of Florida, but had to learn my way around the ghostly realm of these same areas. This was the interesting and fun part of writing this book. I found that people were generally very co-operative and willing to answer my questions, and they were surprisingly receptive in the Fernandina and Jacksonville Beaches areas. Of course beach people are a little different than other people—usually more open and adventurous. Maybe because they live in resort areas and are exposed to many different cultures and lifestyles, it makes them more receptive to ideas different from their own. I had been to these areas many times while growing up in Jacksonville, and found it quite intriguing to visit as a "ghost hunter."

Many Conquerors

Florida itself had many conquerors, unlike a lot of the Northern states, which pretty much had the English as original conquerors. Florida kept changing flags as different countries tried to lay claim to the New World. Not until it officially became one of the United States did any of this transform the State of Florida to its modern-day status. The Spanish were the most predominant conquerors, but the British and French also tried to establish colonies there. At one time, even a former senator from Pennsylvania aligned himself with a French pirate to claim part of Florida for Mexico. What were they thinking?

On top of all that, the Native Americans, mostly the Seminoles, did not go easily into submission. From ancient times, there were the Timucua Indians who held onto this tropical peninsula for thousands of years. That all changed when the Europeans made their way to the New World. The Timucuans were mound-builders and there is very little of their history left. The mounds were burial sites for the different clans and tribes affiliated with the ancient Indians. It is thought the Timucua were part of the Muskogee tribes. Crystal River, Florida, has a state park that is dedicated to the study and preservation of these mounds. Carbon dating has determined these mounds to be from 500 BC to around 1400 AD.

St. Augustine Haunts

I spent most of my formative years just a stone's throw away from St. Augustine, Florida. As a teenager, my friends and I drove to St. Augustine for the fun and sun and little else. I never for one minute, dreamed I would one day be writing a book about the ghosts of St. Augustine and wasn't even aware then, that there were any. Now it is called one of the most haunted cities in the United States. As you will see, it's for a good reason.

St. Augustine is built on a geographical intersecting grid with water running underneath and around it. This creates the energy that a ghost uses to manifest from the spirit realm. There are many stories that abound in this Ancient City and I have tried to find a new slant on some of the old stories, with some new and interesting tales from these same areas.

Having grown up in Florida, the beach areas were a major part of my life. People can be caught in undertows. A dangerous part of the sun and fun is not knowing how to get out of it. On top of hurricanes, tornadoes, sinkholes, rattlers, moccasins, spiders, and just plain old bugs, Florida has a constant battle between man and nature. Not to mention the occasional ancient alligator. Oh, and ghosts...

Fortunately for us ghost hunters, though, people still flock here to build, live, work, and die. To leave their imprint on the land and the spirit world around us.

So, join us as we travel Florida's coastal areas in search of the spirits that live on.

Introduction

I have believed in the survival of life after death ever since I had a near-death experience, or NDE as they are so commonly called, over forty years ago. I know without a doubt there is no such thing as death, as we know it. The soul survives in a place and time of its own. We call it the spirit world. Some call it Heaven, some call it Nirvana. But we end up in the same place, nevertheless.

No one has ever given me a good explanation for what the soul is or where it resides; some say our earthly bodies are the shell for the soul and our bodies become spirit when we die. I also have learned that, as spirits, we can manifest any type body we wish to have. Most people when they arrive in spirit use the body they were happiest with. I have done many years of research on life after death and can only tell you for sure that we do survive this earthly plane. Our friends and family can stay around us in the spirit realm. As spirits, they can even help us from time to time, and if needed, warn us of danger. Death is nothing to fear. It is life here on earth, with all its trials and tribulations, that is the difficult part.

Ghosts have a unique situation all their own. I have had my own ghostly experiences and have never been afraid of them. They can be frightening to people who don't understand them, but they are almost never lethal. Only scary at times, and maybe that is the idea of the whole thing. Perhaps the ghosts could be perpetuating this myth of fear, depending on the personalities of the ghosts themselves, when they inhabited their earthly bodies.

I started each section of the book with a little history of the areas I've covered. Knowing the history helps one to understand the varied nationalities and different ghostly apparitions in that area. St. Augustine is the oldest continuously inhabited city in the United States and was under many different flags. Jacksonville was also under several different flags as were the other cities in Florida. The Spanish flag was the predominant one of the state for many years, until Florida finally became a part of the United States of America.

There is a tremendous variety of ghosts in this book and they include everything from pirates to housewives. Most of the ghostly tales have to do with violent deaths, but some ghosts just like to hang around. Take a journey with me into the past and have fun with my tales of ghosts and pirates.

Fernandina and Amelia Island

A Short History of Fernandina and Amelia Island

As far as a colorful history and many flags flown over it, Fernandina and Amelia Island can rival St. Augustine for that title, starting with the Timucuan Indian mound-builders, which go back to around the year 1000 until the early 1800's, according to the historical records of Fernandina. Although there is evidence they were here much longer, there is no recorded European influence in the area.

The Native Americans had the island and the surrounding areas to themselves, calling it their island paradise, Napoyca. After the Europeans started coming to the land, and fighting over it is when the troubles really began for the Native islanders. The Europeans, as conquerors, brought war and pestilence to the Americas, which helped decimate the Native population.

In 1562, the French explorer, Jean Ribault, was the first recorded European to land on the island, now called Amelia. He named the island Isle de Mar. In 1565, when the Spaniard Menendez drove the French Huguenots from the island, it was then named Isla de Santa Maria. The Spanish established a Mission in 1573 on the island and called it Santa Maria. The mission was abandoned by the Spanish when they were ordered by Spain to relocate it. The mission remained abandoned until 1685, when the British were raiding Georgia. The mission of Santa Catalina de Guale from St. Catherine's Island in Georgia took it over. The mission was abandoned again during the British-Indian war in 1702 when Florida was invaded by Governor James Moore of South Carolina. Governor James Oglethorpe of Georgia renamed the Island Amelia, after King George's II, daughter Princess Amelia (1710-1786), who died as an unmarried spinster at age seventy-five.

The island kept changing flags until eight different national flags had flown over the island.

During one time period, the flag of Mexico flew over the island when Ruggles Hubbard and a former senator of Pennsylvania, Jared Irwin, joined forces with the French pirate, Luis Aury, to conquer the island from the Spanish and lay claim to it for Mexico. They were no match for the United States Navy though, which drove Aury and his forces off the island. Not until March of 1862, when Commodore Samuel Dupont invaded the island, did the American flag start to fly over Amelia Island—and it is still there to this day. The town of Fernandina was platted in 1811 and named after King Ferdinand VII of Spain.

Amelia Island and Fernandina have the old Victorian homes and atmosphere of another time and place. A lot of old towns have these homes, and with it comes a friendly and welcoming feeling in a unique and colorful area.

The beaches are beautiful and are kept immaculate by the park service and the City of Fernandina. You have the clean, sugar-white sand and can watch the shrimp boats and freighters off shore.

One can sit there and enjoy the blue ocean and the warm sun—and do absolutely nothing, for just a little while, along with the ghosts that inhabit the area and still roam the beaches, homes, and hotels on the island.

The Amelia Hotel & Suites

1997 South Fletcher Avenue
Fernandina Beach, Florida 32034
Phone: 904-261-5735

The Amelia Hotel and Suites is a charming little hotel that is located just off the beaches area in Fernandina Beach. It is only a short walk to the beach and is quite comfortable and has easy access to anywhere in Fernandina. I totally enjoyed my stay and the innkeeper was a charming southern lady from Savannah. This is a ghost story encountered while staying at the Amelia Hotel from an unlikely source.

There are no stories of hauntings in the hotel itself, but an employee who works there lives in a haunted house in the Fernandina area. Her mother just happened to be there the day I checked in and I was talking to the desk clerk about my research in Fernandina. The lady overheard my conversation and she proceeded to ask me, "How does one know if there is a ghost in your house?"

My reply was, "Oh, you would know!"

Then she told me the following story:

She said they hear footsteps when no one is there. Her son-in-law, who is living with them, one night decided that he was going to catch her son, who he believed was making the ghostly noises. He heard the footsteps outside the door in their hallway area and when he looked, there was no one there. They have water faucets that turn themselves on and doors that close on their own. She owns a home in the Fernandina area, and I knew then I had come to the right place. The lady also asked me how to find out who was haunting the house? I told her to go to the county records department and check out any previous owners. She said they remodeled the house when they moved in and it seemed to her an elderly or handicapped person had lived there before them. The bathroom area had a place for a person who may have had a physical problem. That is all she could tell me in the short time I talked to her, but that was enough to convince me she did indeed live in a haunted house.

One never knows where you might encounter a ghost story. The people staying at or working in a hotel environment often carry their own stories with them. Or a ghost could become attached to someone who is walking around next to you. Maybe a spirit is strollling the hotel corridors or watching you as you make your way along the road to a beach area. Always keep your eyes open, because you just never know!

The Palace Saloon

The Palace Saloon.

The corner of 2nd Street North and Centre Streets
Fernandina, Florida
Phone: 904-491-3332

The building that houses the saloon was constructed in 1878, and the bar was opened in 1903. During prohibition, there was a brothel upstairs and the shrimp boat fishermen smuggled the booze to the bar owner, needed to serve his patrons. Aldolphus Busch from the Anheiser Busch Company helped design the old forty-foot-long bar. The bar room has an inlaid tile floor and the ceiling is the old-fashioned tin ceiling. The bar fixtures are caryatids (draped female figures), although these may be undraped figures. The bar is lit with old-fashioned gas lamps and the walls have six commissioned painted murals. The atmosphere

Charlie's Room at the Palace Saloon.

is friendly, and when I was there, an elderly black man was playing a harmonica and selling bags of homemade cookies and boiled Cajun peanuts. Naturally I bought the boiled Cajun peanuts. He was quite a character himself. One of the men at the bar told me the old harmonica player sometimes sits in with the band.

A Ghostly Bartender

The haunting of the place is by a former bartender named Charlie. He apparently hung himself in the back bar of the building. They now call it Charlie's Room. He shows up sometimes in the mornings when they are setting up the bar and has been seen by some of the employees. When one of the barmaids saw him, she ran terrified out of the room. A former bookkeeper who worked for the saloon saw him one morning and decided she was not coming back to that room, either. Sometimes the beer taps will come on by themselves. Charlie will sometimes open a closed door, but he appears to be very friendly and just likes "hanging around" the old tavern again.

In 1999, fire destroyed all the upstairs area, except for Charlie's old apartment.

The old Palace Saloon is one of the older historical buildings in the Fernandina area and I would recommend a trip there, if you are ever in the area to check out haunted places, or even if you're not.

The Bosque-Bello Cemetery

14th Street
(One mile north of Atlantic Avenue)
Fernandina Beach, Florida

A trip to any old town would not be complete without a side trip to the old cemetery. I happened upon this cemetery by accident and decided to look around. There was an old part of the graveyard that was established in 1798—I took lots of photos. There was a large stone statue of an angel that reminded me of the cemeteries in Savannah, Georgia, with a lot of moss-draped trees in the area. Right in the middle of the cemetery was a street marker sign. I don't think I have ever seen one *in* a cemetery before.

The name Bosque- Bello comes from the Spanish words for beautiful woods—an apt name for the peaceful and serene atmosphere of the place. Although the cemetery was founded in 1798, the first recorded grave is from 1813 of a French soldier by the name of Peter Bousissou de Nicar. With the cemetery as old as it is, there are many different nationalities buried here.

Some of the inhabitants include the Sisters of St. Joseph, Catholic nuns from France who founded schools in the area and tended the sick during a yellow fever epidemic in 1877. They share the cemetery along with: A Revolutionary war soldier, a Sicilian immigrant, and an African-American family, whose descendants still live in the area. Of course there are many more since the cemetery was expanded over the years.

While I was there, I had a tranquil and soothing feeling about the area, and I felt the spirits looked forward to returning to their final resting places, after they had been out wandering about—with a street marker to guide them back to their graves along the way.

Opposite: **Bosque-Bello Cemetery**

AZALE

The Florida House Inn

The Florida House Inn

20-22 South 3rd Street
Amelia Island, Florida 32034
Phone: 800-258-3301

The Florida House Inn is a large blue painted building in the downtown area of Fernandina, and is Florida's oldest surviving hotel. Opened in 1857 by the Florida Railroad, an interesting assortment of people have visited the place. Among them was, Ulysses S. Grant, the Cuban Poet and Freedom Fighter, Jose Marti, Henry Ford, Mary Pickford, Laurel and Hardy, and many members of the Rockefeller and Carnegie families.

I was able to take some photographs outside and inside the building. It seems as if the rooms downstairs go on forever. When I was there, one of the ladies working there told me that another employee had seen the ghost of a young boy walk by one day.

Another story is that there was a séance in the building at one time and the medium who performed it said the Florida House Inn was a meeting place for spirits. She said that it had a welcoming atmosphere and was comfortable for the spirits who visited. I would say that all of Fernandina is comfortable and welcoming.

The inn is a unique old building with a lot of history. If you're in the area, stop by to take a stroll through the place and maybe enjoy a quiet lunch, or stay in one of the rooms upstairs. Who knows, maybe a ghost or two will drop by during your visit?

The Ash Street Inn & Spa

102 South 7th Street
Fernandina Beach, Florida
Phone: 904-277-6660

Cursed...

One of the places I was told about that had a story to it (though I could not verify the information) was the Ash Street Inn and Spa. It may only be a rumor or local folklore, but the story is of a curse on the family that comes from the infidelity of an ancestor. No one I talked to seemed to know what the story was about, or maybe they just aren't talking? At any rate, this is the tale:

One of the first homes built on Fernandina Island was built by a young couple and the husband had a severe jealous streak. Maybe for good reason. Apparently, he came home unexpectedly one day and things just did not look right to him. Maybe they just look guilty because he subsequently murdered his wife and his best friend. Now there is a curse on the family that has lasted for five generations.

The curse is in the form of a triangle shaped pigmentation mark on their foreheads and goes into their hairlines. There's a white streak that goes through the hair. Doesn't matter that it might be genetic. The story still circulates about the curse on the family.

The house that was the scene of the murders is still standing, though and is now a bed and breakfast. Stop by for a stay at the Ash Street Inn; just keep a close eye on your forehead and hair just in case the curse does not extend to the family only!

Fort Clinch State Park

2601 Atlantic Avenue
Fernandina Beach, Florida
Phone: 904-277-7274
(open from 9 am to 4:30 pm)

Having heard the stories about the haunting of Fort Clinch, I had to see the old fort for myself. The tour guide who accompanies you through the fort has been plucked right out of the eighteenth century and relocated to Fort Clinch. He is a colorful and interesting character and makes the tour itself quite an attraction.

He won't admit to any hauntings in the fort, but never mind. None of the State Park services personnel ever will—no matter where you go. My guess is that part of their indoctrination is: Don't admit to any ghost or hauntings.

At any rate, there still persists the stories of the haunted fort. One tale is about the ghosts of the Union soldiers who still join the re-enactment of the battles fought in the fort.

The re-enactors of today perform the same duties as the soldiers during 1864, at the time of the Civil War. They do the everyday tasks of maintaining the fort during that time period, along with any Civil War battles that may have ensued.

Fort Clinch served as a military post during the Civil War and the Spanish-American War. During World War II, the Coast Guard, Army, and Navy used it as a surveillance and communications post.

There are various islands in the area and the Coast Guard kept watch along the beaches to keep spies and saboteurs from landing on our shores. Not a bad history for a fort that was never officially completed.

Some people have heard a baby crying in the southwest tunnel area. That story comes from a time in the 1920s when, supposedly, a homeless family stayed at the fort for a few months. They lost a baby girl while they were living there, when she died of a serious illness.

Some people have seen a lady in white (maybe wearing a nurse's uniform). They did have a hospital at the fort where surgery was performed. Women usually were not allowed in the fort after dark, but as a spirit, who can stop her?

Another of the stories is of a Union soldier who promised his wife in a letter that he would return from the war. Evidently he didn't, as he is still haunting Fort Clinch, waiting to get home to his wife. It has been said that when the staff or volunteers stay overnight, they can hear unexplained footsteps about the place that just may be his.

The construction of the fort was started in 1847 but was never totally completed. The wall around the fort is where the tunnels are

located and there are several old brick buildings inside the fort itself, which lends to the atmosphere of the place. There is an officer's quarters but the officers themselves stayed in town, only coming to the fort by boat to conduct business during the day.

One story the guide tells is of a man who spent time in the solitary confinement cell. They were very serious about solitary confinement in those days. The cell is very small with no windows and dark as night inside. It only has a small slot in the bottom for food or water. The prisoner somehow managed to escape. But he was recaptured and tried for the crime. His attorney got him off on a robbery charge. It seems he had stolen over $200 in Confederate money from a southern woman. Because Confederate money was not considered legal tender, his attorney was able to get that charge dropped, but they did get him for desertion, and he was executed for that crime.

After he was dead, they buried him in a black-painted coffin, face down in an unmarked grave.

Desertion was a very serious crime back then, and there was no going to Canada to escape. You would have more than likely been tracked down and returned to your small, dark cell to await execution—the same way the doomed escapee did, leaving a ghostly imprint upon the place he worked so hard to escape from.

Ft. Clinch State Park

Amelia Island Museum of History (The Old Jail)

Amelia Island Museum (The Old Jail)

233 South Third Street
Fernandina Beach, Florida
Phone: 904-261-7378

A Pirate Hangs

The Amelia Island Museum of History started life as the Old Nassau County Jail in Fernandina. The haunting of the building comes from the 1700-1800s eras.

The specter is of a man named Luc Simone Aury who was the illegitimate son of the pirate Luis Aury, born Louis-Michel Avery in Paris, France, sometime around 1788. Luis is the old pirate who tried to claim Fernandina for Mexico. His son, Luc, was an outlaw in his own right, who committed murder, rape, robbery, and other heinous crimes against his fellow man. He was eventually captured and sentenced to hang at the Nassau County Jail. The day before the public hanging, Luc Aury decided to slit his own throat, rather than be hung as a public spectacle. A doctor was summoned to stitch him up so that he could still be hung at the public gallows. The "ceremony" scheduled for the next day, and a huge crowd was gathering for the hanging of the notorious criminal.

Obviously the doctor was in a hurry and not too worried about how he stitched up a man who was scheduled to die anyway, because when he was hung, his head was almost severed from his body and blood spewed all over the crowd which was gathered in front of the gallows.

There was instant panic in the crowd. Women fainted, men screamed, and children were trampled when the panicked crowd fled in terror, trying to get away from the gallows. Old Luc Aury can still be heard moaning where the gallows used to be and when he appears, it is with a gash in his throat that is covered in blood.

The first floor of the current museum is where the old jail was located and where the hauntings occur.

If you want to know more of the history of haunted Fernandina, see the Ghost Tour sponsored by the Museum by calling 904-261-7378. It starts in the cemetery behind St. Peters Episcopal Church at 801 Atlantic Avenue, Fernandina.

Amelia Island Lighthouse

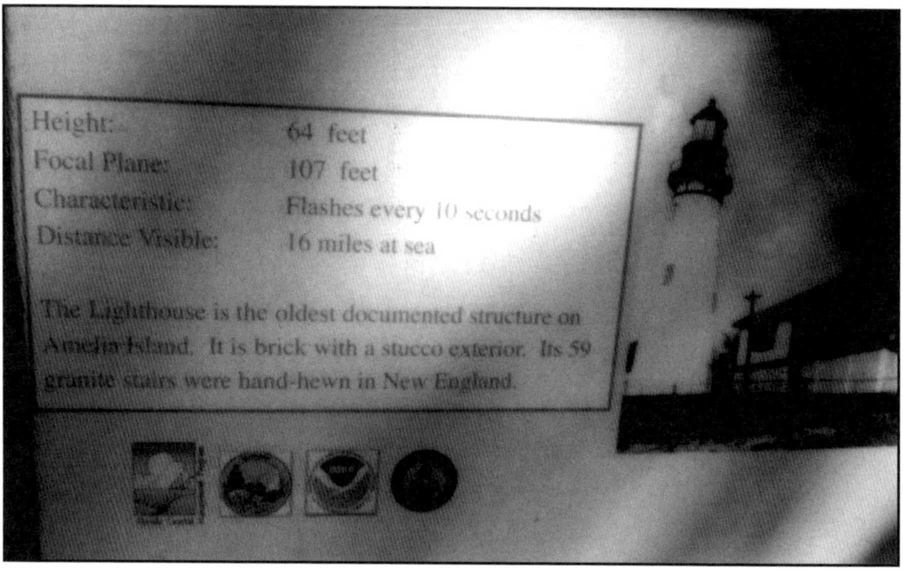

Height: 64 feet
Focal Plane: 107 feet
Characteristic: Flashes every 10 seconds
Distance Visible: 16 miles at sea

Amelia Island Lighthouse

Exit 373 off I-95 to SR 200
To Amelia Island entrance off Atlantic Avenue
Amelia Island, Florida
Phone: (City of Fernandina) 904-277-7350

Although I did not get a chance to tour the lighthouse, I am including it anyway. I was able to get some photos of it on my way to Fort Clinch. There are several viewing areas and they do have tours scheduled to the lighthouse itself.

The lighthouse is supposedly haunted by a former lighthouse caretaker and his wife. It seems he took his young bride to live at the lighthouse and she died a tragic death. He was so distraught that he hung himself at the top of the lighthouse. People can sometimes smell putrid odors and a radio comes on by itself every night and locked doors are constantly unlocked.

Amelia Island, before Congress took over in 1821, was the gateway to the Southern states for the black market slave trade along with smugglers, drunkards, and prostitutes. With the long history of violence in the area, is it any wonder ghostly activity would extend to the lighthouse? Maybe a lighthouse keeper or two looked the other way to allow a few of the unsavory characters of that time to slip by. Would a guilty conscience, perhaps, keep someone attached to this world?

It does happen.

The Kingsley Plantation

Kingsley Plantation

On Fort George Island
A1A/105 just north of the Ferry landing
Web Site: www.nps.gov/Timu

In 1803, Zephaniah Kingsley relocated to Spanish Florida and became a successful merchant. In 1806, he purchased his African wife in Havana, Cuba, from the Senegal area of Africa. Anta Madgigine Jai, was a thirteen-year-old slave when they left Cuba, and she was pregnant with her first child by Kinsgley. Kingsley freed Anna (Anta) and their children in 1811, which meant that she and her children were considered slaves for five years. Anta (now known as Anna) then moved with her three children, and her slaves, into their own plantation house in Mandarin.

After uprisings began in Florida in 1813, Anna and Zephania were back together, and moved to their home in Fernandina. Zephaniah Kingsley moved his family to Ft. George Island in 1814. Anna had her own house built on the plantation grounds and she was her husband's business partner. Her house is adjoining the main house and was built because the customs of her heritage dictated that she should have her own home. She was a freed woman and owned her own slaves who were housed on the plantation grounds.

The old slave quarters are Tabby houses and are located on either side of the gates, just as you enter the plantation area. It is rumored that Zephaniah Kingsley also kept his other wives and slave mistresses in these quarters. Kingsley, who was a law unto himself, had multiple wives and children, the same as the men did who came from the Senegal area. Anna, coming from the African nation of multiple wives was able to adapt to the situation, but she remained the number one wife, caretaker, and matriarch of the family. She outlived her husband, Zephaniah, and ended her days in Florida on property owned by her daughter and her daughter's Dutch husband, near the Pottsburg Creek area. She is buried in an unmarked grave on the property.

Having left her home in Senegal and captured as a slave who was sold to Kingsley, Anna Kingsley still managed to live a full and prosperous life here in the United States, running plantations of her own and enjoying the riches of a husband who was a wealthy merchant seaman with ships and extensive properties in the southern states.

Slave Murder

The rumors of haunting on the plantation stem from a murder that was committed by one of the slaves. When he was captured, he was hung by the front entrance of the plantation in an old oak tree. They say he is still there and people swear they have seen his eyes watching them. But who knows? Maybe it is only an animal's eyes glowing in the dark. How do you prove or disprove the feeling of someone there watching you, though?

In 1837, due to the harsh laws enacted in the state of Florida against freed slaves and blacks, Kingsley moved his wife Anna, their two sons, and fifty freed slaves to Haiti, which was a free black republic. Their two daughters remained in Jacksonville, married to wealthy white men. When Kingsley died in 1843, he knew his family would be safe and secure in Haiti. His wife Anna, still returned to Florida to end her days there with her two daughters.

Singing Ghosts

Kingsley Plantation has a past that encompasses the many changes going on in Florida during that time in history. I would imagine the slaves who lived on the plantation were treated much better than most of the blacks during that era, but they were still kept as slaves both by Zephaniah and his wife Anna, a former slave herself.

The stories of hauntings relate to people driving onto the plantation after hours on a back road into the area close to the old slave quarters. It is said that if you drive in and park your car, then sit there for awhile, you will hear the sound of the singing of old slave spirituals. If you stay too long, strange things will happen to your car and it will start to shake. It would be to your benefit to get out of there as fast as you can. I certainly would not want to antagonize the ghostly slaves while they were singing their hymns...

Jacksonville, Florida

History of the Jacksonville Area

The earliest known history of the area is 12,000-16,000 years ago when the forerunners of the Timucuan Indians inhabited the area. The Timucuan, who at one time numbered close to 150,000, disappeared when the Europeans came to Florida in 1513 and brought disease and war. By 1763, the Timucuan were almost completely eliminated from the state of Florida.

When Ponce De Leon landed twenty-five miles south of Jacksonville, he was looking for the Fountain of Youth. After establishing the area for Spain, he sailed off again on his fruitless mission, but not before naming the area Pascua Florida for the Spanish Feast of Flowers when he had landed in April 1513.

In 1562, Jean Ribault of France claimed the area and in 1565, the Spanish regained the area. The British controlled Florida for a while, and when the Treaty of Paris ended the war with England and her thirteen North American colonies, Florida was again ceded back to Spain, but sold to the United States for five million dollars in 1819 as part of the Adams-Onis Treaty. To put things in today's perspective, one piece of beach property in California alone, can sell for five million dollars.

Jacksonville Escapes

Jacksonville escaped the land battles fought during the civil war years with only one battle fought between the Union Soldiers and the Confederate army by a Union ship in the river and the Rebels in the St. Johns Bluff area.

In 1791, Jacksonville was named Cowford due to the shallow water in the river where cattle were driven across. In 1822, when Andrew Jackson became the first military governor of Florida, the name of the town was changed to Jacksonville. Andrew Jackson later became the seventh president of the United States.

Burned to the Ground

On May 3, 1901, the entire city was destroyed by a fire that started in a mattress factory during lunch hour. A spark from the kitchen area started the blaze in the mattresses which were filled with Spanish moss and quickly spread when it exploded. Winds picked up the burning moss as it spread from one wooden rooftop to another. The whole city burned to the ground in eight hours. Destroyed in the fire were 146 city blocks, 2,368 buildings and the fire left 9,000 people homeless. Amazingly, only seven people died in the fire.

The Confederate Memorial in the Hemming Plaza in the middle of Jacksonville escaped destruction, although witnesses say the base of it was glowing red.

The port city was quickly rebuilt, and by 1912 , 13,000 buildings had been constructed, and the railroad that Henry Flagler owned, was making a major impact on the area. The city government also took over the port area. By then the St. Johns River had been dredged to make it deep enough for ships to enter the port terminals that were along the river front in the downtown area.

After consolidation in 1968, which made Jacksonville at that time the second largest city in the world in land area. The mayors of Jacksonville started their own reconstruction of the city. That is still going on to this day and Jacksonville has become a cultural and beautiful city of the South, with lots of added features going for it, rising like a Phoenix from the ashes of destruction from the fire of 1901.

Mayport, Florida

The William Joseph King House

The William Joseph King House Mayport

Corner of Ocean & Roxie Streets
Mayport, Florida
(Private Residence)

Mayport Village was founded in 1562 and is an old, dilapidated small fishing village. Shrimp boats come in with their daily catch of fish and shrimp, to sell to the local restaurants and warehouses. Not much in the way of improvements in the area in quite a few years, that I could see. There is a lighthouse in the area, but it's behind a chain-link fence, that appears to be government property. With the area staying as it is, the haunted tales flourish.

There is an old brown two-story house in Mayport with a history of hauntings and a lot of colorful stories to go with it. The original house was built in 1865 and burned in 1905. It was rebuilt in 1913 by William King.

A retired Jacksonville attorney living in the house now is restoring it to its original condition. If you decide to visit the house, the *Beware of Dog* sign is a valid one. He has four big dogs that live there with him and they take their job of security seriously. Do not open the gate and try to go in. The attorney is the only one who can control them.

Brothel Stories

The house is sufficiently creepy looking and I can easily see why it has a reputation of being haunted. From what I could gather, the house, when it was rebuilt, was built on top of an old Mayport brothel. There is a tale that the madam of the brothel was mad at a little red man (probably a native Indian) and she stabbed him in the stomach with a pitchfork, then carried him over her head and out into the street where she dumped him.

There are also stories of bodies being thrown into the ocean and washing up on the shores in Jacksonville Beach and no one knowing where they came from. I can easily see that the stories would go along with a brothel in the area and especially during prohibition. It would take the Jacksonville police over an hour to get to the Mayport area and that is plenty of time to get rid of almost anything. Bodies or evidence of a crime.

When I was given a short tour of the house, I was shown a photograph of a woman who was a psychic medium standing in front of a huge painting and there is definitely a face showing up in the photo alongside, where she is standing. It is a misty-looking face superimposed on top of the painting itself. The Attorney showed me a photograph taken of him with his granddaughter and there are spirit lights in the background of the photo over their heads.

He told me that Duke University did a "ghost hunt" experiment there and definitely found a "presence" in the house.

Poltergeist

I interviewed a young man named Keith, who had spent some time there when William King's brother John Franklin King, owned the place and he said there was definite poltergeist activity in the house. He said a girl in a long white dress was seen at the top of the stairs and there was the sound of a child crying in one of the bedrooms. Things would also be moved around in the house.

I also talked to a Jacksonville mailman who used to visit the house when John King owned the place. Evidently he liked the company and was not afraid to let people come for a visit any time of the day or night. Maybe Mr. King felt safe with the ghosts and knew people were already sufficiently scared anyway.

He told me that sometimes when you would go to visit the house, it would be a mess—the blinds off the windows and things in disarray. He said they would go visit the cemetery and come back, and everything would be straightened up and in order. He told me there was no way, Mr. King would be able to get things in order in the short time they would be gone. He also told me about a car being moved once when he was there. It had been left locked in front of the house, and when they got ready to leave, it had been moved back from the original spot where they had left it to down the road from the house. Do ghosts move cars as well as objects around the house? It seems if they can clean house and move cars at the same time.

The Homestead Restaurant

The Homestead Restaurant, Jax Beach, Florida

1712 Beach Boulevard
Jacksonville Beach, Florida
Phone: 904-249-9660

The Homestead Restaurant sits on land that was a Spanish land grant conceded to Don Juan McQueen in 1792. Mr. McQueen was the character in a novel by Eugenia Price entitled *Don Juan McQueen*. After passing through numerous ownerships, the property was acquired by Mrs. Alpha O. Paynter. The building itself is an original two-story log building which was built in 1934. In the beginning, the log home was used as a private residence. It became the Homestead Restaurant in the late 1940's.

Mrs. Paynter used the home not only as her private residence but as a boarding house. In 1962, Mrs. Paynter sold the building to Preben and Nina Johansen. Mr. Johansen who also owned the Le Chateau was a prominent restaurant owner in the Jacksonville area for many years. The current owners are the daughter and the family of Preben and Nina Johansen. Supposedly, Mrs. Paynter is buried on the property behind the old restaurant.

Once a Hostess, Always a Hostess

The haunting of the restaurant is a colorful and interesting story of a woman who still welcomes guests into her home after many years of being long gone from this world. Once a hostess always a hostess, it seems.

Mrs. Paynter is the ghost that haunts the restaurant these days. She appears to be a very active spirit and has been seen and photographed by a few people. Ghost Tracker Investigations spent several nights in the restaurant and were able to pick up spirit activity in the building.

I talked to a couple of people and found that the spirit activity has not ceased. Mrs. Paynter appears to keep a hand in the operations of the restaurant still. Although at times, somewhat in a disruptive manner.

There is one particular room that seems to have the most activity. It is a small dining area off to the right as you come in the front door. The employees had come into work one morning and found all the tables moved around and the china broken and scattered over the floor.

There is an upstairs area that has no plumbing, yet water leaks from the ceiling above onto one of the tables in the restaurant area below.

A couple of people have seen a likeness of Mrs. Paynter in the restaurant. When they describe who they have seen, it is the same as a picture of her they have upstairs.. She has been seen sitting next to a young girl in the restaurant and once standing in front of a fireplace in the building.

The employees told me that recently, one morning, they came in and tables and chairs had been moved outside! Now that would be a major poltergeist achievement. I would love to have seen that one myself with the ghostly inhabitants carrying tables and chairs outside the restaurant. Maybe dinner with a ghost outside is in order!

Pete's Bar

Pete's Bar, Neptune Beach, Florida

117 First Street
Neptune Beach, Florida
Phone: 904-249-9158

Pete's Bar is almost a landmark in the Jacksonville Beaches area. It has been there as long as I can remember and many people have been in and out of that bar during the years. Pete Jensen, the original owner, was a World War II veteran. There are photographs and mementos of him scattered throughout the bar itself. There are two main bars, a pool room, and a back bar area.

The bartender who is working there now has been there for quite a few years and knows a lot about the bar and people who have been customers over the years—although he is very discreet and would not mention any names, even if you asked him. He is a perfect bartender, I would say.

Jumping Photograph

The bar itself lends the right atmosphere for a haunted building. The only poltergeist incident I could get out of anyone was from a young lady who works there part time cleaning the bar. She told me that one day she was cleaning as usual and apparently she was doing too good of a job, and a photograph of Mr. Jensen jumped off the wall at her. He kept the place neat, but I would imagine he also wanted a little bar odor about the place. Not bleach or cleaning solution.

They say his spirit stays around the old bar area, and since it still bears his name, he more than likely still feels that he maintains ownership. Only from the spirit realm now.

The Atlantic Theaters Comedy Club

751 Atlantic Boulevard
Atlantic Beach, Florida
Phone: 904-249-7529

Rumors of hauntings sometimes just won't go away as in the case of the Atlantic Theaters Comedy Club in Atlantic Beach. The comedy club started life in 1964 as the Royal Palm Theater.

The haunting of the club started with the robbery and murder of a projectionist who used to work there. People sometimes see a black shadow walk by and a man in a beige shirt in the projectionist's booth after hours at the club. The manager has had chairs moved around. After it was checked out by a ghost hunter, she quit writing up one of the employees, who she thought was not putting them away as she was supposed to. Having seen the phenomena for herself, she finally realized the resident "ghost" was moving the chairs out after they had been put up for the night.

Jean Ribault Monument

Fort Caroline Road
Jacksonville, Florida (Fort Caroline area)
Part of the Timucuan Preserve

If you take a drive down Fort Caroline Road towards the Fort Caroline area, you will see a sign directing you to the Jean Ribault Monument. The granite monument sits high on a bluff overlooking the St. Johns River and has a view worth driving up to the monument for. If you go there alone and sit by the monument, you may feel a strange vibration. I have visited the monument twice by myself and the first time was when my mother was dying of leukemia and congestive heart failure. Their home was not far from the area and it seemed a place of refuge at the time. The first time I visited the monument I had a feeling of great peace and comfort. Maybe because I was seeking this while there. All I know is I felt a powerful vibration around me and it stayed for quite a while.

The second visit wasn't quite as comforting. I had a feeling of danger nearby and did not stay long.

A Bloody Past

The history behind the Ribault Monument and the Fort Caroline area is a bloody one between France and Spain. Both nations were trying to gain territories for their own countries in the New World.

There was a shipwreck just a little north of St. Augustine that changed the course of history for Florida and the French in this country.

Jean Ribault, the French explorer, had been released from a London prison and was sent by the King of France, along with 500 French soldiers to rescue the French Huguenots in the Fort Caroline area and to help maintain a French colony in Florida.

In the meantime, a Spanish explorer by the name of Pedro Menendez de Aviles was building a fort and training his soldiers in St. Augustine. He was determined to rid Florida of the French presence once and for all.

The Jean Ribault Monument, Fort Caroline

When Jean Ribault tried to sail into Florida to rescue the Huguenots who were still there, a sudden severe storm destroyed his ships. What was left of his men were stranded on a beach just north of St. Augustine. Menendez marched north with his army of 500 men and captured Fort Caroline, which had been established by Ribault's men years before. When he came upon Jean Ribault and his remaining army, he slaughtered them. Menendez's soldiers took the French soldiers behind the sand dunes a few at a time, and if they did not convert to Catholicism, they beheaded the French soldiers unmercifully.

Vibrations

With the violent history of the area itself, it isn't any wonder there are strong vibrations at the monument that represents the French people who were eventually killed by the Spanish. There was still a French Huguenot presence in St. Augustine though, as the Huguenot cemetery attests to.

Standing at the monument sometimes you can feel the fear of the people who had been slaughtered there. It's such a strong physical sensation, that it makes you want to run away as fast as you can.

I am not the only one who has had that feeling of extreme fear. A good friend of mine, who is also a sensitive, had the same reaction to the place. The strange part, is that it comes and goes. Not always the same feeling every time.

A Haunted Home in Jacksonville

Fort Caroline area
(Private Residence)

There is a home in the Fort Caroline area of Jacksonville that is haunted by the mother of one of the owners of the house. The older lady has a tendency to open closed doors and just wander in.

I have been there a couple of times myself when this has happened. You will be sitting there talking in the kitchen area, and suddenly, for no reason, the back door will open by itself. The wife just looks up and says "B" is coming in, as if it were an everyday occurrence. And it does happen on a pretty regular basis.

On an updated note, I was talking to the widow of the former owner of the house, who recently passed away, and just as I mentioned his name, the back door just blew open—only there was no one there. The family was getting ready to construct a memory garden at their home, and I feel as if he was there to supervise and make sure they did it exactly right.

One time the granddaughter saw her grandmother sitting at the kitchen table. She saw her the way she looked when she was younger and before she had a tragic accident that somewhat disfigured her. She said she saw her grandmother just sitting there, but nothing was communicated to her.

An Elephant for Your Thoughts

Since they had been good friends of my mother's, she used to visit them occasionally after she died. They knew it was her because she would ring the elephant bell they had on a kitchen shelf. Once, she even knocked a plate off the shelf. My mother had a rather extensive ceramic elephant collection, and people would bring her elephants back whenever they traveled somewhere. Ceramic, clay, or anything an elephant collection could be made of, she had it.

My mother and dad were circus performers with the Ringling Brothers Barnum & Bailey Circus many years ago, just before World War II . One of the things my mother did was ride the elephants around the arena during the opening parade. She even had her own favorite elephant, Cass, who unfortunately, died in a tragic circus fire one year.

Right after my mother died in 1998, I was living out in the country. I had walked to the back of the property and laid down in a rope hammock. I was next to a natural creek in the area and the sound of the water and birds was very peaceful.

Suddenly, the hammock started rocking back and forth very gently. There was no breeze that day and I was not moving. I had the strong feeling it was my mother who had come by to rock me gently, one more time.

I stayed there for quite a while just enjoying the sensation of being rocked again like a small baby and feeling my mother's presence.

Old Coast Guard Station Museum

24th Street and Atlantic Avenue
Jacksonville Beach, Florida
Phone: 904-560-7500

This old coast guard museum is haunted by at least two ghosts. The first one is an old surfer who is often seen in the tower.

The second ghost is a sailor whose ship was torpedoed off the coast of Florida during World War 11, and his body stayed in the coast guard station for a short while until it was moved to the morgue. His presence is usually felt rather than seen.

Photos that people have taken at the museum show orbs, mist, and other strange things.

The Vanishing Hitchhiker

Girvin Road
Jacksonville, Florida

One day a woman who had heard stories of the vanishing hitchhiker decided to check it out for herself. She and her daughter drove out to Girvin Road about 2:00 AM in the morning. They drove for quite a while, trying to summon up the ghostly spirit.

They came around a curve in the road and there she was, standing on the side of the road. She appeared to be moving in slow motion and was trying to get their attention so they would stop for her.

The apparition apparently frightened both the woman and her daughter and they quickly left. Later she called the Jacksonville Ghost Hunters Society, and when she described the girl, who was also wearing glasses, she was told that it fit the description of the girl who haunts the area.

Ghost Light Road

SR 210—St. Johns County
Switzerland, Florida

The ghost that haunts the Ghost Light Road area is a motorcyclist. He was decapitated by running into a rope or heavy string that was strung across the road by teenagers playing pranks on people. He must have been going pretty fast to have lost his head in the accident, but according to St. Johns County police, that is what actually happened.

Motorists would say that you could drive along the ghost Light dirt road and one bright light would come at you, then suddenly vanish. And if you looked behind you, one red tail light would be going away from you.

This phenomena has been seen by quite a few eye witnesses, including teenagers quite frequently, since ghost hunting is a favorite past time for teenagers. But you have to be driving only five miles per hour to see it happen.

Some people think this is lights from an intersection nearby, but the people who have seen the phenomenon have said that, from a distance, it wasn't lights at all. Rather, it was only one bright white light coming towards them on a dark and lonely night with no one else around—being scared out of their wits as the light approached them, then quickly disappeared...

The Haunted Day Care Center

Near Cecil Field
Jacksonville Naval Air Station
Jacksonville, Florida

Karen Russell, a member of a paranormal society in Jacksonville told me the story of a day care center where she worked for several years. She started working there in 1999 and said that every so often she would hear a child's laughter in the back of the room. And when she went to check it out, no one was there. She didn't share this information with anyone else, and it went on until 2004, when employees were told the building was being sold and they would have to vacate the premises.

Activity Escalates

That is when the spirit activity escalated. By this time, the Assistant Director of the day care was aware of the child's spirit laughter. Now, instead of one child, it was three children laughing in the back of the building. Other people working there started questioning as to whether there was anything unusual going on in the day care. They started sharing stories of hearing unusual things when no one was there and would smell perfume or a man's cologne.

Not willing to scare the day care workers away, Karen just let them think it was their imagination. Then one night during a staff meeting, they all heard the sound of children laughing in the building, and when they ran back to check, of course, no one was there. After that, Karen told them what had been happening and they were all okay with it and no one felt threatened.

Towards the end of 2005, the laughter increased, the smells became more predominant, and they would see shadows in the room or outside on the playground. Then some of the children at the center started to see and hear things. One little girl had a spirit friend who would sit next to her and they would carry on a regular conversation. None of the children had been told about the spirit visitations, but children, are usually sensitives anyway.

A few of the teachers still refused to believe anything odd was going on, but one night two of the teachers were locking up and heard the sound of the children's laughter and when they went to check, no one was there. The one teacher who did not believe in any of this, felt a child's soft touch on her cheek. That immediately changed her mind about the whole thing!

At the beginning of 2006, they were told the building would be sold in June and the spirit activity stepped up even more. One time, they saw a spirit woman and child on the playground watching the other children while they were playing. A few times, they saw a man and smelled his cologne. When they came in, at times, in the mornings, the toys would be scattered around the room as if children had been playing with them and left them there. Once they even heard a child crying.

In March of 2006, Karen called TAPS (The Atlantic Paranormal Society), a phenomena investigation agency, and had them come out to see what was going on and maybe why the spirit children were there. The medium who was with them said a little girl about six years old had been run over by a car when there was a dirt road outside of the building. She was grounded in the building and other spirit children would come play with her at the location, after regular day care hours. There were also other visiting spirits and that was why there was so much activity in the building.

Shadows and More Ghosts

A lady named Vicki Barrett worked at the day care center and had come in on a Saturday to pick up some laundry. She heard a little girl softly crying in the back of the day care. She said she heard it off and on for about three minutes.

She has also seen the black shadow of a little girl very clearly. The child would enter the room wearing her hair in curly pigtails and had on a pinafore-type of shift dress. She would walk along the wall and stand behind the teacher. Then she would look at Vicki and nod to her, while she was standing behind the teacher. Vicki also saw the little girl out in the playground area with an older woman just watching the other kids playing.

The other spirit she saw, towards the end of the time before they had to move out of the day care, was a tall man dressed in business attire. He had his jacket off and his shirt sleeves rolled up. He had taken his tie off and was pacing back and forth, appearing to be agitated. He wore his hair in the slicked-back style of men from the fifties. She saw him in the room where the three year olds were cared for, but the room was empty, as they had already moved things out of the building.

A few times when she would be in the kitchen by herself fixing lunch, she would get a creepy feeling and have to leave the room. The pantry had a sturdy latch on it and she would slam it shut and make sure it was latched. When she returned, the pantry door would be wide open. The door could not open by itself as the latch would stay latched once it was closed. Or at any rate, until a spirit decided to open the door.

Just remember to be careful if you decide to close a business that has occupied an old building for a while, because you just may be stirring up some long-gone spirits that have become attached to the place.

21

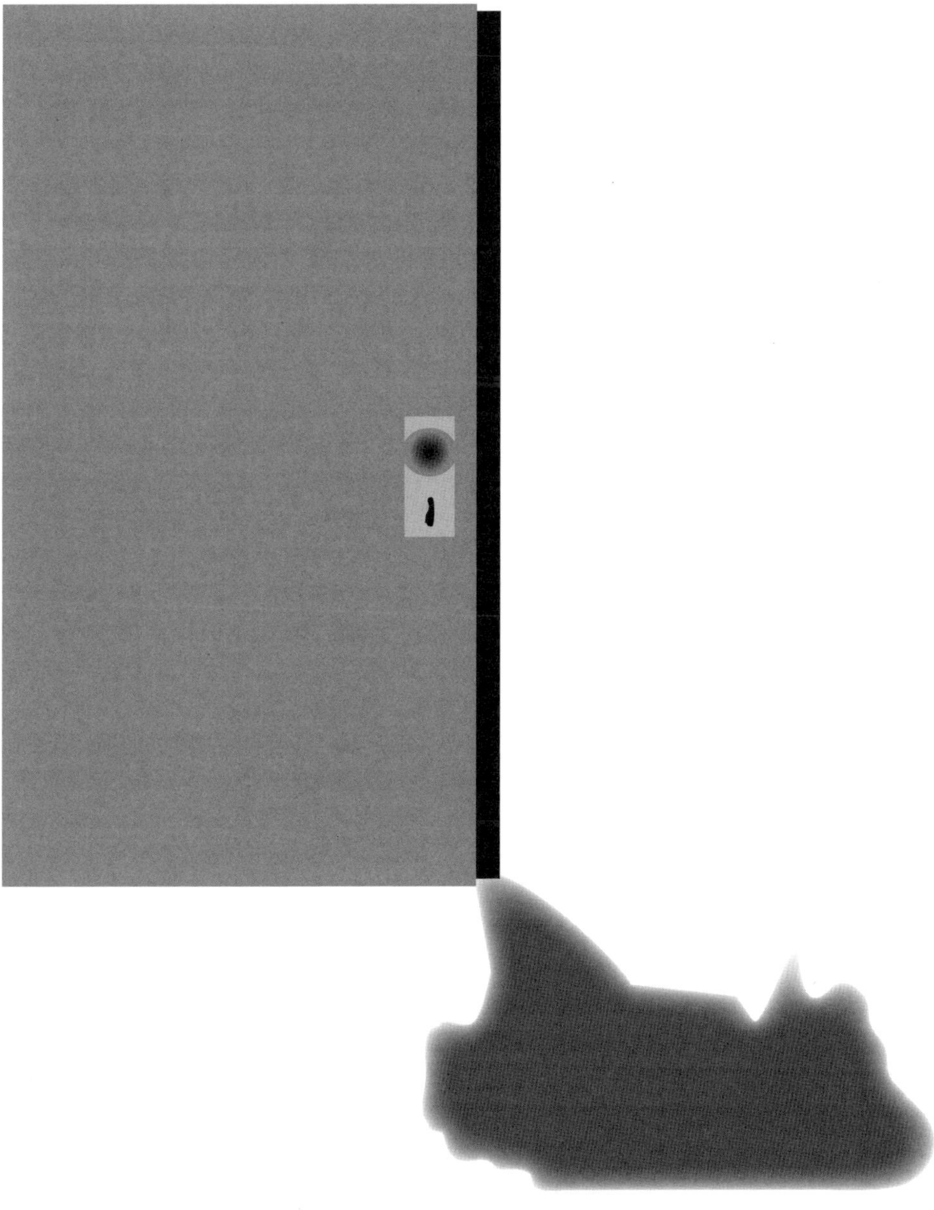

The Trout River Ghosts

Jacksonville, Florida

There is a home located on the Trout River across from where an old fort used to be located, that was built around the year 1902 or even earlier. It was built near or on top of an area where the burial grounds for some mill workers were located. Stacy, who is a member of the Jacksonville Paranormal Investigation Society says this home belongs to her mother and that she grew up there. As a young girl (twelve or thirteen) she could see the spirits and no one would believe her. Not until they showed up in a photograph, that her mother once took of her beautifully landscaped yard, did anyone take her serious.

The spirit she saw when she was younger, was of a man who appeared to be digging in the yard next door to her. He would dig over and over again in the same spot. She now feels it is a residual spirit, as he keeps doing the same thing over and over. (A residual haunting is a psychic imprint that is repeatedly played out and seen by someone living. The spirits in these time warps often seem unaware of being observed by others.) He is a large man who glows white and just keeps digging. She couldn't tell if he was digging for treasure or digging a grave.

The photo also shows a different man who appears to be in period clothing, maybe from one of the Spanish wars that were fought in that area. From the time of the Spanish Explorer Menendez, until the French and British were driven out and the Native Americans were conquered, Florida was a constant battlefield.

If you should happen upon a ghost who is acting strange, maybe repeating the same thing over and over again, just remember they are not even aware you are there watching them. The image is stuck in a time frame it can't seem to get out of, or there is a psychic imprint left on the area that will just stay there. I think it would be similar to a shadow on a wall that isn't a real thing, but the image is still there and that is real.

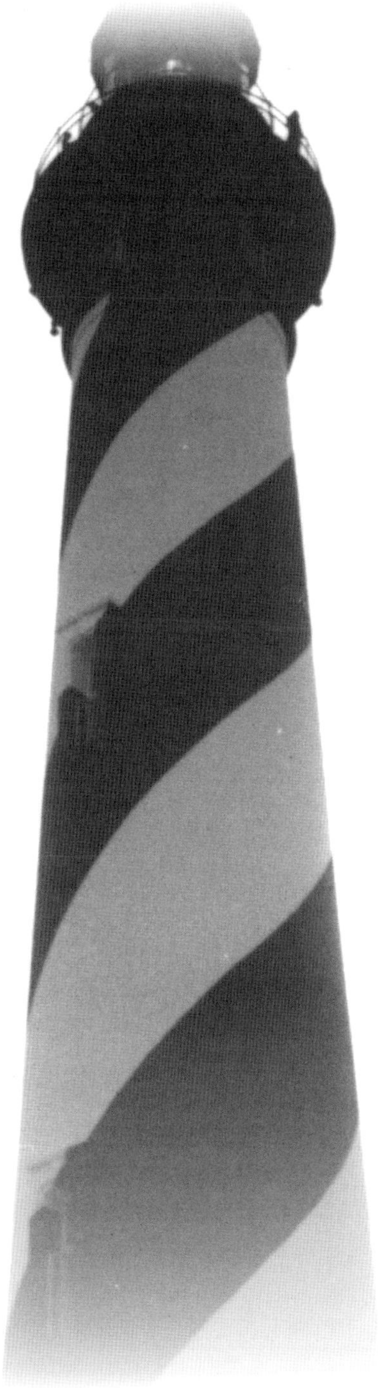

St. Augustine

A History of St. Augustine

In order to understand the many hauntings of the city of St. Augustine, you have to know some of the background and the history of the area itself.

St. Augustine was first established as a Spanish Colony on September 8, 1565 by Pedro Menendez de Aviles. He was also the first governor of Florida and is now buried in Aviles, Spain, a sister city of St. Augustine, Florida. The other sister city of St. Augustine is Cartagena, Colombia.

The colony of St. Augustine was established as the oldest continuously-occupied city in the United States.

St. Augustine has a violent history and a varied past with five different flags having flown over the city during the many years of occupation. The first flag to fly over St. Augustine was during the First Spanish era which began in 1565. In 1586, Sir. Francis Drake laid siege to the town and burned the city. Then in 1668, pirates plundered the city and killed most of the residents. The first Spanish era lasted for over 297 years.

More Flags

The second flag to fly over the city started in 1763 when the Treaty of Paris ended the French and Indian wars and Florida was given to the British government; thus began the British rule over St. Augustine. Britain was able to govern the area that it had been unable to capture due to the establishment of the Spanish Fort (Castillo de San Marcos) which was completed in 1695.

The fort was actually built to protect the city against pirates. During the time the city was under British rule, it also coincided with the American Revolution, which lasted four years. Florida stayed under British rule for twenty years.

In 1783, another Treaty of Paris was signed, which gave Florida back to Spain and that lasted from 1784 to 1821 beginning the second Spanish period in St. Augustine's history, and the third flag to fly over the city. This second Spanish rule lasted for thirty-seven years.

In 1821, St. Augustine and Florida became a territory of the United States by the Adams-Onis Treaty when Spain was defending itself against Napoleon, who was trying to conquer all of Europe. Spain at that time sold Florida to the United States. Trying to govern an area in the new world an ocean away, would have been more than Spain could deal with at the time, and I'm sure the money paid to Spain for the state of Florida helped in Spain's war effort against Napoleon.

Officially a U.S. State

In 1845, Florida became an official U. S. state, which began the fourth time a different flag was flying over the city, but in 1861 Florida seceded from the union and became a Confederate state with the fifth flag being the Confederate one flying over the fort. Because of the old fort and it's strong military use, the Union was able to regain control of Florida on March 11, 1862, when it captured the fort and Florida remained under Union control until the end of the four-year Civil War between the states.

In 1865, Florida re-joined the United States and has remained under that final flag ever since.

More Violence

Unfortunately, the violent history of St. Augustine did not end there. During the civil rights era, St. Augustine became a battleground again.

The Ku Klux Klan and segregationists battled for control of the city. Martin Luther King, Jr., Ralph Abernathy, and Andrew Young all led demonstrations there during the volatile time of the civil rights actions. Some say the confrontations helped establish the Civil Rights Act in 1964.

With all the different cultures that were established in St. Augustine, one can see why there is a variety of ghost stories to tell.

Today, things are much more peaceful except for the occasional murder every small town in America seems to have to deal with. Then again, if it wasn't for that and people dying of disease, accidents, and old age, there would be no more ghost stories to tell.

The Old Jail Museum

Sheriff Joe Perry, Old Jail

167 San Marco Avenue
St. Augustine, Florida
Phone: 904-829-3800

Driving into St. Augustine from US Hwy 1 and turning left off the highway into the town area, I never intended to stop at the Old Jail Museum. As it turned out, I stumbled into my first haunted area by chance. During the tour, the guide, "Deputy White," who is dressed in authentic western clothing from the turn of the century, was a very credible guide to that era. He made the tour itself interesting, and entertaining to someone who wasn't expecting much.

The admission fee was only $6.00 and worth it. I learned a lot about law and order, or lawlessness and no order, in this small town in Henry Flagler's time. Henry Flagler was the money behind the building of the Old Jail. Originally, it was located close to the mammoth hotel he was constructing, but he didn't want his guests to be exposed to the criminal element of the that time, so he had it moved.

Since Henry financed the building of the jail, he wanted (and could afford) the best. It was constructed to resemble a hotel, and housed seventy-two prisoners with the sheriff's living quarters adjacent to the jail itself. The jail was built by the same company that built Alcatraz. Guess Old Henry wanted to make sure there would be no escapes.

In the late 1880s, the total cost to buy the land and build the jail was $20,412.35. Cheap by our standards of today. The jail was opened in 1891 and was still used sixty years later—which says a lot about the construction of the building itself. (Although I can't imagine a sheriff actually wanting to live in his small quarters after housing started improving in this country. It would have been as confining as the jail itself.)

Hanging Aplenty

Many a criminal was hanged out behind the jail and this was a major social event of the day. People would gather around whenever a hanging was scheduled. The prisoners could view the hangings along with the town folk since the hangings were directly behind the jail.

There were no screens or glass on the windows and cold weather and rain came through, with no protection at all for the prisoners from harsh weather. They *were* criminals after all. At least, that is the way they were perceived back then. No amenities whatsoever. If one of the prisoners fell ill, they were not separated from the healthy prisoners. That could have been the sheriff's way of economizing. Let them die and not have to worry about feeding them any more, or as a form of prison population control. Not that prison food was worth living for.

Women and men were housed in the same jail, but in a different area and the kitchen was stifling. The women prisoners did the cooking and it was mostly beans and greens with a little hardtack (unleavened bread made into large hard wafers) that had to be softened in black coffee before anyone could eat it or bit into it. It was called hardtack for a very good reason.

The Old Jail, St. Augustine, Florida. Lights appear around Deputy White quite often when photographyed.

Innocent and Dead

I'm sure there was more than one innocent person who died in that jail, and not by hanging. Dying would have been the easiest way out of there. A lady psychic who visited the jail said she encountered a prisoner who was hanging around because he was afraid of where he would go besides where he already was. He let her know he was not guilty of the crime he was hung for, but had not led an exemplary life and was afraid he would go to hell.

You get a really creepy feeling when you visit the area where the prisoners were kept before they were taken out to be hanged. Not a pleasant experience at all. There are dummies lying around to look like prisoners, and even *they* look sad. One employee said he had seen an apparition disappear through a wall near the jail area.

The tour guide who plays the role of Deputy Guy White, a man who was murdered in 1911, says he has seen the ghost of a man who wears a cowboy hat in the jail area. He told me that one night he was walking downtown to collect money from a man who owed him, and walking next to him was the ghost cowboy. When he first saw the old cowboy, he was standing in front of a door at the old jail and there was a woman standing with him who had done the tour. When the cowboy walked by, he had to catch the woman before she hit the ground in a dead faint.

Still Hanging Around

When the jail opened, the sheriff was Charles Joseph Perry—Florida's most feared sheriff. He was a huge man, standing 6'6" tall and weighing over 300 pounds. When you visit the part of the jail where the sheriff and his family were living. It is connected right next to the jail itself, you wonder where his poor wife slept. The bed was only big enough for him. The rooms are very small and the sheriff's desk is still there in his office in the downstairs part of the home. Life for his family had to be very interesting back then. The children, I'm sure, never got bored. How could they? Hangings, murderers, thieves, and no telling what other scoundrels lived right next door.

Sheriff Perry spent many years there and some people think he still "hangs around" to keep an eye on the place.

When I photographed the jail as "Deputy White" was setting up the tour, a strange light appeared in one of the photos and Deputy

White says people often say they have lights around him when their film is developed. My developed film showed up with a huge orb and there are other lights that appear in photographs taken in different parts of town especially at a murder scene on Marine Street and the Spanish Military Hospital on Aviles Street.

With spirits disappearing into walls and cowboy ghosts wandering by, no wonder someone falls over in a dead faint once in a while.

Flagler College

(Formerly Ponce De Leon Hotel)

74 King Street
St. Augustine, Florida
Phone: 904-829-6481

Hotel Days

Traveling around St. Augustine, you can't help but notice the Flagler hotel, built by Henry Flagler, who was an oil baron from the turn of the century. He co-founded the Standard Oil Company with John D. Rockefeller, so he had the money to build anything money could buy. The hotel is magnificent in the old world style of architecture. It takes up two city blocks and now is a co-ed college that has students living in an opulence, probably not experienced by most of them in today's world.

Henry Flagler spared no expense in the construction of this huge hotel. It was officially opened on January 10, 1888. Travelers arrived by train and were taken at dusk to the hotel so they could see it glittering with the newly-installed electric lighting. The guest list included Ulysses S. Grant and Frederick Vanderbilt. Hundreds of people were entertained by grand balls in the magnificent ballroom with two orchestras playing overhead on balconies at either end of the large room.

I can imagine the amazement of the guests as they arrived to see this large opulent hotel in the middle of a small town in Florida. St. Augustine is not a large city anyway, and back then it was even smaller. How Henry Flagler managed to construct this magnificent building during that time is a minor miracle in itself. Of course he did own the railroads which helped him get any materials he needed quickly and probably a lot cheaper, too.

College Days

The hotel changed hands to become a college for women in 1968. With Henry Flagler's history of problems with women, I can just imagine what his ghost must think of that? Henry's second wife, Ida Alice Shourds Flagler, came to St. Augustine with him, and some say she is one of the spirits who still haunts the hotel/college. They say she haunts the dormitories on the third floor east wing which were her private quarters before she was committed to a mental institution where she lived until the end of her life. Ida Alice Shourds Flagler had been Mary Harkness Flagler's nurse during Mary's illness, before she died. Mary was Henry's first wife, and the mother of his children.Mary died when she was just forty-seven years of age.

Mary Harkness was a frail lady, who was still able to bear Henry three children. Henry married Ida Alice two years after his adored first wife, Mary, died. Ida Alice had a short stint as an actress before she turned to nursing. She was married to Henry Flagler during the time he built the Ponce De Leon Hotel. Some say she was a big influence in his decision to build the hotel, using St. Augustine as her means to the social life she was denied in New York.

Henry had Ida Alice committed to a mental institution in New York when she was in her early fifties. Isn't that is the age most women are going through menopause? It used to be the general consensus that women were going crazy during that time. I remember asking an older woman once, when I had reached that age, what women did before hormone therapy? She said they were committed to mental institutions. Wouldn't your husband having an affair with a much younger woman cause one to have temper fits and irrational behavior? Me thinks the lady was set up!

Maybe haunting the old hotel is Ida Alice's revenge after all.

Ouija Troubles

Apparently, Ida Alice was interested in the Ouija board and listening to what Spirit was telling her through the board. Was Spirit telling her what old Henry was up to? She had already been sent away one time because of the Ouija board and when she returned home, "someone?" gave her another Ouija board. That looks mighty suspicious to me. The story is that she stabbed the doctor on the way to the mental institution with a pair of scissors. Why would a doctor let a mental patient have access to a pair of scissors as he was taking her away? If she wasn't really insane, maybe she decided she had nothing to lose and was taking her anger out on the doctor? It would certainly make me crazy to be committed to a mental institution, all the while knowing, it was all a ploy by your husband to get rid of you to marry a much younger woman, and that her family was well paid to help keep her there.

If you go to the Internet and look up Ida Alice Flagler, you will find some interesting tales of friends and relatives raiding the endowment, that was set up for Ida Alice by Henry, after she was sent off to the mental institute. Some of the stories are beyond belief.

I would imagine that Ida Alice considers the old Ponce De Leon Hotel/Flagler College to be *her* hotel. Maybe she still *is* wandering the halls?

Once Ida Alice was committed to the mental institution, Henry then changed his residency to Florida where he was influential in getting legislation passed to divorce a person who, after four years, is considered incurably insane. Which would have been timely for him. He then married a woman who was thirty-seven years younger than himself, Mary Lily Kenan, a prominent North Carolina Socialite. Henry was then 71 years old and his health was beginning to fail. Mary Lily would have been in the prime of her life.

Hotel Hauntings

Stories of hauntings at the hotel began with Flagler's funeral in 1913. He died after a fall down a flight of stairs when he was eighty-four years old and living in his palatial home called Whitehall, that he had built for Mary Lily in Palm Beach, Florida. Do you think maybe an angry spirit could have given him just a little shove down those stairs? Henry, with all his money and endowments, was a scoundrel after all. I'm sure he had his share of enemies—both living and dead. When he died, Mary Lily would have been just turning fifty—the age where menopause usually sets in.

Supposedly a likeness of Flagler is embedded in one of the postage stamp-size tiles in the main entrance. The story is his spirit was trying to escape and bounced off a closed window and landed on a small tile near the back of the room to the left of the doors. This tile is very hard to find because it is so small.

The story is that Henry's spirit flew around the rotunda, and the large double doors blew open to let him out. His body is entombed in the Flagler Memorial Presbyterian Church behind the old hotel. (More about the church and it's hauntings later.) After Henry's spirit exited the building, the huge doors to the rotunda slammed shut. I can just imagine him making the kind of exit that would get people's attention.

Henry Flagler Statue

More Haunting Tales

These days, ghost tours stay outside the building on the sidewalks to tell the stories of hauntings in the old hotel/college. The college discourages ghost stories about the building, since they feel it would scare potential students away.

Several stories abound about who is haunting the building. One is that Henry Flagler had a mistress at the hotel, when his third wife, Mary Lily, returned home unexpectedly. He apparently locked his mistress in a room on the fourth floor and kept her there. A very small room with no windows. She was claustrophobic and hung herself in that room.

A young lady visiting a student friend of hers in one of the third-floor dormitories, was alone in the bathroom with the door locked. She spotted a young woman in a white or light-colored dress with long brown hair in the mirror as she stood up from leaning over. When she turned around, no one was there and the door was still locked.

Later, as she was sitting on the bed talking to her friend, her friend's cell phone rang with her guest's phone number appearing on the caller ID. The guest had left her phone in the bathroom to re-charge while she was visiting with her friend. Looking for the cell phone, they found it still on the charger in the bathroom where she had left it. Who was trying to call while they were on the bed talking? Could it have been the lady in white experimenting with the modern day phones? That would be my guess. Spirits like to play with water faucets, electrical outlets, and electronic devices.

One young man whose sister attended the college says she has heard strange voices in her room and one time "someone?" blew in her ear. Objects have been moved around, or have disappeared, only to be found later in odd places.

Supposedly, the objects are moved around by a small boy named James who haunts the building on the third floor west wing. He slams doors when he is in a bad mood, and occasionally, they can hear a ball bouncing in the halls and a tricycle being ridden. When anyone opens the door to check out the noise, no one is there.

There have been rumors of a lady in a blue gown who haunts the stairs leading to the dining area. Supposedly, she fell down the stairs while she was pregnant killing herself and her unborn child. We all know how clumsy pregnant women can be, with one's balance thrown off by the big belly in front.

Some people claim to hear orchestra music coming from the fourth floor which may have been used as a ballroom. Others say it was a solarium, not a ballroom. But why couldn't you play music in the solarium? It makes sense to me, playing music in a solarium.

Spirits may still be having their balls and parties in the old hotel, while the students are asleep in former hotel rooms, that are now their dorm rooms.

Flagler Memorial Presbyterian Church

Flagler Memorial Presbyterian Church

32 Seville Street
St. Augustine, Florida
Phone: 904-829-6451

The church is a beautiful structure that was built next to the college. Visitors are welcome and there is no charge to view the sanctuary and the tombs of Flagler and his family. There is a donation box available for anyone interested. When you enter the church, you get a feeling of sanctity. The building has been well preserved by the parishioners.

Henry Flagler built the church in memory of his daughter, Jennie Louise Bennett. It was constructed in the Venetian Renaissance Revival style and modeled after the St. Marks in Venice. It took a little less than one year to build and was finished in 1890, while Flagler was still married to Ida Alice. It was said to be the finest and most costly house of worship south of Washington, D. C.

Henry Flagler is entombed in a crypt along with his first wife, Mary Harkness Flagler. She and Henry were married for twenty-eight years, before she died of illness. His daughter Jennie Louise who died at age thirty-four, due to complications following childbirth, is in another coffin. She and her child are buried together in the same coffin. You can see these coffins behind a large gate that opens off the inside of the sanctuary.

His other daughter, Carrie, who died at age three and his only son Harry Harkness Flagler, are not in the crypt area. Henry's son, Harry, did not choose to follow in his famous father's footsteps and it caused a lifelong rift between them. There was an argument when Harry was working for Henry in one of his companies. After that, he left the family and never spoke to his father again. I'm not sure whose idea it was to not have him or his other sister buried there. Maybe Harry himself? Also missing is his second wife, Ida Alice Shourds Flagler who died in the insane asylum in New York years after Henry died—even though Henry was married to her when the church was built and, according to records, the church was conveyed in his and Ida Alice's names. She may be missing from the crypt in the church, but not the nearby hotel.

Henry Flagler is said to haunt the church on Seville Street. He has been seen by a couple of people walking down the aisles in the church between the church pews. Maybe he is still trying to redeem himself in the afterlife?

Ripley's Believe It or Not Museum

Ripley's *Believe it or Not* **Museum**

19 San Marco Avenue
St. Augustine, Florida
Phone: 904-824-1606

The Ripley's Museum started life in 1887 as a winter home for Walter G. Warden and his family of sixteen. He was an associate of Henry Flagler and was partner with John D. Rockefeller and Henry Flagler in the Standard Oil Company. Additionally, he was President of St. Augustine Gas and Light and was Director of the St. Augustine Improvement Company. His home was built by the same firm that built Flagler's home. The Warden family stayed in the home until 1925. After that, the house stayed vacant until it was purchased by Norton Baskin, who was married to Marjorie Kinnan Rawlings, writer of The Yearling and Cross Creek that was a Pulitzer Prize winning novel in 1939. Both were both made into movies.

A Fire Trap

When Norton Baskin and his wife, Marjorie, remodeled the home and it became The Castle Warden Hotel in 1942, it had twenty-five guest rooms. Marjorie Rawlings Baskin still had her home in Cross Creek and spent time there while Norton was away. He was an ambulance driver with the American Field Service on the India-Burma front from July 1943 until October 1944. Marjorie was at Cross Creek when a good friend of hers, Ruth Hopkins Pickering, and another young lady in her twenties, Betty Neves, from Jacksonville, were staying at the hotel. While they were visiting, a fire broke out on the third floor. Even though Ms. Pickering was on the fourth floor staying in the penthouse suite that belonged to Ms. Rawlings, she and her friend, Betty Neves, both died of smoke inhalation. The hotel was repaired and re-opened within a matter of weeks. The Baskins sold it in 1946.

In a letter to Norton Baskin, among Marjorie Rawlings memorabilia in the Smathers Library at the University of Florida in Gainesville, she tells of her tremendous grief and guilt over the death of her friend at the hotel. The penthouse had been declared a fire trap. No doubt that was the reason the hotel was sold soon after the repairs.

One of the bellhops tried to save the women, but was unable to because of the heat. He said he heard Mrs. Pickering screaming at her window. Can you imagine the terror that woman must have felt at being unable to flee a burning building? She stood looking out at the world that would have been a safe haven just outside her window, with the knowledge that she was about to die. No wonder she still haunts the place!

People claim to see a ghostly figure at the windows from time to time, and when they check, no one is there. Is Ms. Pickering still trying to get out? A staff member of Ripley's Museum has seen a woman in the penthouse with medium-length hair and wearing a robe or a gown.

The hotel was sold to the Ripley family in 1949 and turned into the Ripley's *Believe It or Not* Museum. Visitors to the museum sometimes hear piano music and an orchestra playing. Lights go off and on unexpectedly and other poltergeist activity happens in the museum.

Too Sensitive?

There have been several paranormal groups and sensitives visit the museum, but the Ripley people feel it stirs things up too much, so they don't encourage it any more.

In August of 2006, a couple of people who are both sensitives, went to visit the museum. They heard the words, "Get Out! This is my home!" The lady at the ticket booth told them it was Ruth who had died in the fire. The wife, who was one of the sensitives, said she experienced tremendous sadness that slowly dissipated as she got further away from the building.

In August of 2002, a group of ghost hunters were allowed inside the building after hours and they set up equipment to detect any spirit activity. With the equipment, they found spirit activity and orbs mainly around the Ferris wheel and on the stairs. One of the ladies became ill and passed out, and when they helped her out of the building, a spirit orb followed her down the stairs.

With the deaths of the two women and all the unusual and weird displays in the building, is it any wonder the place is haunted?

St. Augustine Lighthouse

81 Lighthouse Avenue
St. Augustine, Florida
Phone: 904-829-0745

You have to cross the historic Bridge of Lions to get to the lighthouse, but it is a drive worth making. It's still a working lighthouse and was constructed at it's current site in 1874. The original lighthouse was built in 1823 but started eroding and the lighthouse area had to be moved. The structure is 165 feet tall and uses First Order Fresnell lens. The beacon visibility of the light is 19-24 miles. It was constructed by Paul Petz, the same person who built the Library of Congress. Driving along highway A1A, the lighthouse suddenly appears on the horizon and looms larger as one gets closer.

At first, the light for the beacon was provided by lard buckets which had to be hauled up the 219 stair steps on a daily basis by the lightkeeper or his assistant (probably more often the assistant). The light keepers had to be in pretty good physical shape to carry those huge and heavy buckets of lard up that winding stairway every day. The height is equal to a 14-story building. Those steps are not for the feint of heart. Even today they have restrictions on who can climb the stairs. If you have heart problems or breathing problems, I would not recommend it. Just looking up at the stairway from underneath it is daunting. After they stopped using lard, the fuel they used was kerosene. Not until 1936 was electricity added.

When you visit the Lighthouse Museum, you have to pass through a building constructed on the grounds for selling souvenirs and information about the lighthouse itself. Then you are outside in a nicely-shaded little park area that you have to walk through to be able to get around to the living quarters. When you can walk through the woods to the lighthouse, you can't see the harbor and it doesn't appear to be a lighthouse area at all. The lighthouse keeper's quarters are located next to the lighthouse—a two-story structure with a balcony that runs across the front of it.

The Junior Service League of St. Augustine has done a tremendous job of preserving the lighthouse and the grounds around

St. Augustine Lighthouse

it. The museum and grounds are kept in immaculate condition and are well cared for. They could write a book on how to preserve lighthouses around the country.

The haunting of the lighthouse itself has a long history to it. Workmen were working on the construction of the light keepers house, and one young man who was helping in the restoration said he saw an image of a man hanging from the rafters. He was told that indeed a man did hang himself there.

A man in Victorian clothing has been seen in the house and a young girl was also seen during the restoration of the house. There are several stories of young girls who have died there, with one of them involving a train in the area.

Little Girl Ghosts

The little girls who haunt the place were daughters of Hezekiah Pity. They were thirteen-year-old Eliza and fifteen-year-old Mary, who were playing there with the lighthouse keeper's daughters while he was working on the new lighthouse in the late 1800s. The new lighthouse was being constructed farther up the island and they were playing in one of the train-carts used to haul supplies up from the bay. The brake came loose and the cart hurtled to the bay below, and before anyone could rescue the girls, two of the four girls drowned in the bay.

These are the young girls who can be heard playing and giggling about the grounds. Their laughter can be heard in the lighthouse itself and Mary is seen in the same blue velvet dress and blue hair bow she died in.

There are also stories about a young girl who was killed by a nearby train and who haunts the area. A report of a young girl wearing a period-type dress has been seen there. The little girl and a woman in white have been seen during the times when there are bad storms at the lighthouse area. With the long history of the lighthouse itself, there are probably many more ghosts and spirits "hanging about" the place.

The people at the museum say the little girls who died there, play on the balcony. At times they are seen or heard running and giggling across it.

One of the light keepers who lived there, Peter Rasmussen, was a big cigar smoker and so was a man who fell to his death while painting the lighthouse. They say they can still hear his footsteps on the stairs below. Sometimes people can smell cigar smoke about the place. But which of these two men, no one knows. Only the cigar smoker knows!

The Basement

The basement area of the old house has the most activity. One of the executive directors of the museum has seen a man walk past her while there. When she called to him, he didn't answer her, then just disappeared. There are also reports of a man wearing a uniform seen down there in the basement.

The Atlantic Paranormal Society (TAPS) has done an investigation in the lighthouse and some of them say they saw the silhouette of a man who was looking down on them from an overhead railing as they were going up the stairs. They chased him and when they got to the top, no one was there—and there was no way out. One of the men had stayed down below them to make sure no one came back down the stairs.

The ghost team also recorded the voice of a female asking for help.

St. Augustine's Lighthouse Keeper's Cottage

Even if you don't believe in ghosts, the lighthouse is worth seeing, unless you are afraid of heights that is! Just maybe you will smell a little cigar smoke or hear a young girl giggle. But watch out for the man on the stairs—especially if you should happen to smell any cigar smoke!

Heritage Baptist Church

Wildwood Drive
U S Hwy 1 south of St. Augustine (church is on the right)
St. Augustine, Florida

Another haunted church in the St. Augustine area is the Heritage Baptist Church south of St Augustine. Sometimes, when the congregation sings "Zion's Hall", the ghost of a former parishioner wearing a black top hat comes in and sits down in the minister's chair during the song. That apparently was his favorite hymn.

An eleven-year-old girl has seen the former minister (who had died five years previously) greeting people at the door as they came into the front door of the sanctuary.

There is a man who has seen, only one time, an image of a huge angel statue in the cemetery hovering over one of the graves.

At one time, two ladies were doing genealogical research in the cemetery, and when one of them went to bed that night, she heard the words "You forgot the one in the middle of Wildwood Cemetery" repeated several times. Sure enough, when the ladies returned to the cemetery, and after determining where the middle of the cemetery was, buried underneath several layers of moss was the grave of Henry O'Barnum with the dates of November 29,1828 - July 25,1880. Mister O'Barnum, who was fifty-one years old when he died, was going to make sure he was not left out of the research.

A Haunted Sea Captain's House

268 St. George Street
St. Augustine, Florida

With the ocean on top of St. Augustine, it would be lacking on my part to not include at least one sea captain's haunted house in this book. This Victorian house was built in 1892 with a ballroom on the third floor. The sea captain's wife used to go up to the ballroom and played the harpsichord for hours while the captain was out to sea.

One night, the lady failed to come down to dinner, and when the servants went up to check on her, they found her dead over her harpsichord.

The house has been converted to an apartment now, and residents can sometimes hear music coming from the old third-floor ballroom.

One former resident, a lady named Bobbie Bay, decided one day, to follow the sound of the music to see where it actually came from. She had been bothered by the music when she was trying to sleep. She saw a lady dressed in a yellow satin gown and heard the music of the harpsichord playing in the background.

She had been accusing some of the younger residents of the apartment house of playing their music late at night and disturbing other older residents who were trying to sleep. She kept going down and checking on them and they would deny each time it was them. She later apologized to them about the accusations after she had seen the woman in yellow and heard the music from the third-floor ballroom. Sometimes, after that, she would leave the door to her bedroom open that goes to the old ballroom area to make it easier for the lady to still go up there to play her music.

Huguenot Cemetery

Huguenot Cemetery

10 South Castillo Drive
St. Augustine, Florida
(Just outside the Old City gates across from the visitors center)

The Huguenot Cemetery was established during a yellow fever epidemic in 1821. It was constructed for the Presbyterian population who were the Huguenots in the area from the time of the French occupation of North Florida. Some of them had left the Fort Caroline area after becoming disillusioned with the French settlement.

One of the ghosts haunting the cemetery is that of John B. Stickney, a judge from the early 1800s. He died in Maryland of malaria, but was shipped back to St. Augustine for burial, since he had spent many years there as a judge and was a prominent citizen of the small town. At Huguenot, they buried him near a big oak tree in the middle of the cemetery. His family decided they wanted him returned to the north, however, and buried in a family plot. But when the gravediggers took a break from digging him up, and returned, they had a surprise waiting for them.

Some grave robbers had an idea that Stickney had something worth stealing. It was only his gold teeth. The robbers were going through his bones and had dug out his teeth and thrown his head across the cemetery when they were confronted by the gravediggers. The gravediggers re-united Stickney with his head and shipped his body back up north to Washington, D. C., where his children wanted everyone buried in their family plot.

Still Looking...

But Stickney still haunts the Huguenot Cemetery looking for his gold teeth. Residents have seen him walking about the cemetery with his head down like he is looking for something.

Other people have been able to photograph white orbs in the cemetery and in the trees. The spirits of St. Augustine are a restless lot.

Another ghost that appears is a headless man who grave robbers had dug up and stolen his head. Evidently, he and his head were not reunited, because he appears to be still looking for it. Why anyone would want to rob a grave is beyond me, but maybe he had gold teeth, too?

Gold teeth seem to be worth keeping. I've heard stories of people stealing the gold teeth out of corpses in the funeral homes or crematoriums of today. I suppose they could easily do that and who would know?

During the yellow fever epidemic, there were children who died and were buried in the cemetery. Some people have seen them still playing in the trees and among the tombstones.

The Huguenot Cemetery is a popular ghost hunting destination for the area's ghost hunters. Many people have photographed the cemetery and have had the orb lights show up in their photos. The spirit activity seems to be most predominate at night. Are the spirits of the children still playing around in the trees and gravestones in the old cemetery?

32

Tolomato Cemetery and the Oldest Drug Store

Tolomato Cemetery, St. Augustine

Cemetery on Cordova Street behind the oldest Drug Store on
31 Orange Street
St. Augustine, Florida
Phone: 904-824-2269

This site was used by the Christian Indian Village of Tolomato prior to 1763 when the remnants of the Tolomato people, along with some of the Spanish, left Florida for Cuba. It was also used by the Spanish Franciscan missionaries, but was abandoned when Great Britain acquired Florida in 1777.

Father Pedro Camps acquired permission from the governor to bury his parishioners on the site of the former village and was himself buried there in 1790. After ten years, he was interred and moved to another burial site.

The Oldest Drug Store. Eerie black cloud over the drug store on an otherwise clear day.

The cemetery seems to be haunted by the spirit of a young boy and several children. They play among the gravestones and up in the trees. A figure of a man has also been seen watching over the cemetery. Could it be the old Franciscan Father Camps still watching over his flock?

Tolomato was a Seminole Indian Chief who was buried in the area. Some say the old drug store is built on top of Indian burial grounds. When I developed photos taken on a clear sunny day, a large black cloud is seen hanging over the oldest drug store area.

There is a story of a woman in a white dress with long, light-colored hair that haunts the graveyard. It is said she can be spotted mostly at 9:20 PM walking among the tombstones. She is the ghost of a bride who died on her wedding day.

When the Oldest Drug Store was constructed in 1739, it was during the time the Spanish were controlling the area—at the time the store owners sold liquor, tobacco, medicine, and Indian remedies. They also concocted their own medicine on the premises, which I'm sure consisted of a lot of alcohol, or even what we would consider today to be illegal substances.

If you go into the oldest drug store you will see a tombstone erected in Tolomato's honor. The wording is rather odd, but says:

NOTIS
THIS WERRY
ELABORTE
PILE
IS ERECKETED IN MEMERY OF
TOLOMATO
A SEMINOLE INGINE CHEEF
WHOOS WIGWARM STUUD ON
THIS SPOT AND SIRROUNDINGS
WE CHERRIS HIS MEMERY AS
HE WOOD KNOT TAKE YOOUR
SKALP WITHOUT YOU BEGGED
HIM TO DO SO OR PADE HIM
SUM MUNNY
HE ALWAYS AKTED MORE
LIKE A CHRISTSUN GENTLE
MAN THAN A SAVAGE INGINE
LET HIM
R.I.P.

St. Augustine National Cemetery

St. Augustine National Cemetery

104 Marine Street
St Augustine, Florida

This national cemetery with a very colorful past is surrounded by the headquarters of the Florida National Guard. Well kept and clean, the grounds almost look like any other military cemetery, except for a few differences. The headquarters for the superintendent was built in the Spanish style of the old homes in the area. It was constructed in 1938, with coquina shell, an overhanging balcony across the second story of the building, and a tile roof. Not your usual headquarters for a cemetery super.

Originally, the grounds was the site of an old Franciscan Monastery. During the British occupation of the oldest city from 1763 to 1783, the British military occupied the monastery and when the Spanish took over from 1783 to 1821, the Spanish military utilized the property and then it officially became a military cemetery.

While photographing the cemetery, I noticed three pyramid-shaped structures on the property. Curious about why they were there, I started doing some research and discovered the varied history of the cemetery.

The first interment of soldiers took place in 1828 during the Indian wars when the Seminole Indians resisted the U. S. Government's attempt to forcibly remove them from their land. The wars lasted for seven years and the Seminoles, led by Osceola, were never defeated.

On December 23, 1835, Major Francis L. Dade and his company were ordered to reinforce General Wiley Thompson's troops stationed at Ft. King, Ocala, Florida. Major Dade became lost during the trek, and it was winter, which can be cold in Florida with the icy wet winds. Major Dade's soldiers were carrying their weapons underneath their heavy coats, which made it difficult to easily get to them. When the Seminoles attacked, they were wiped out, except for two soldiers who managed to survive. Someone had to tell people what really happened.

In 1842, when the fighting finally ended, the Army gathered the bones of all who died in the territory during the fighting to oust the Indian population, including Major Dade and his soldiers. They are buried in the three vaults, which explains the three pyramids in the cemetery. The bones of 1,468 unknown soldiers are also underneath the pyramids. Nearby, there are several plain-white markers designating the graves of Seminole Indian Scouts.

Wouldn't you imagine that with all the graves and unknown soldiers buried at this cemetery there has to be some ghostly spirits hovering about trying to find their way home?

When I first saw the photograph of the black cloud over the drug store, I had a very negative reaction to the photo. My feeling is there is a lot of negative energy in that particular area. It could be because of the burial practices of the Spanish people and the neglect of the Indian burial grounds.

While I was checking out the cemetery, I had the distinct impression of a Monk-type figure in the area of the supervisors' building on the premises. When I walked over to an area that seemed to have some type of podium, I felt a strange energy and had the feeling that, as a woman, I was intruding in an area where women were not allowed. I made my getaway while I still could.

Athalia Ponsell Lindsley

124 Marine Street
St. Augustine, Florida
(Private Residence)

The ghosts of St. Augustine would not be complete without the story of Mrs. Athalia Ponsell Lindsley, the murdered wife of the former mayor of St. Augustine. On January 23, 1974, she was killed with a machete in broad daylight in her own front yard. Athalia had been a former Powers model and socialite from Jacksonville, Florida. Her life had been intertwined with the Kennedy family and she was a well known and controversial figure in St. Augustine.

Murder in St. Augustine

Athalia's next door neighbor, Alan Stanford, the county manager, was arrested for the murder but not convicted, even though all the evidence pointed in his direction. Her other neighbor, who was an eighteen-year-old boy at the time, told his mother that he saw Mr. Stanford "hitting" Athalia in the front yard.

Almost all the people who were involved in the case are long dead and gone, but I think Athalia's spirit still hangs around the area. If anyone has a right to haunt a place, she does.

A major injustice was done to her and her only crime was that she was a woman who was ahead of her time. She was outspoken and contentious, but with a conscience that would not let her look the other way when she felt things were not going the way they should. Athalia was a staunch environmentalist and fought for what she believed in, even when her life was threatened. Which it had been, by Alan Stanford.

St. Augustine was divided over the murder trial and, to this day, some people feel she "got what she deserved." It has been said that if you want to commit murder and get away with it, you can do it in St. Augustine. Well, I have heard the same thing said about small towns in Tennessee and Georgia. So, St. Augustine does not have a monopoly on that one.

Athalia Lindsley's murder has been well-documented in a book written by Nancy Powell and Jim Mast entitled, *Bloody Sunset in*

Athalia Ponsell Lindsley

St. Augustine. Nancy was the Bureau Chief in St. Augustine for the *Florida Times* Union at the time, and a good friend of Athalia's. She moved in the same circles as Athalia and knew all the people involved in this grisly crime.

Another murder was committed on Marine Street ten months after Athalia Lindsley's murder. An elderly woman, Frances Bemis, and possible witness to the Athalia's murder was beaten to death as she took her nightly walk around the Marine street area. That murder was never solved either.

Justice Not Served

Athalia Lindsley has never received the justice she deserved, but life has a way of creating its own form of justice. Alan Stanford had to leave the area after the trial, and as of January 2007, he was living in another state and still maintains his innocence. No one actually believes him and there are still web sites dedicated to proving his guilt.

Athalia is probably still bitter about the outcome of the trial where Alan Stanford was able to walk away and she had to die, leaving an imprint of violence on her much loved house and yard.

Do Photos Tell?

I took a photo of the house and area where Athalia's body was found and there is a strange light in the area where she was murdered. I'm thinking Athalia is still there, waiting for justice to be done.

The Pirates of St. Augustine, Florida

The stories of Florida would not be complete without some of the history of the pirates of that ancient peninsula. Pirates have long found the coastline of Florida an attractive port of entry for their activities.

A man the Spanish considered a pirate in 1565, named Sir John Hawkins, sailed to the northeast coast of Florida to rescue the French Huguenots with the help of a Frenchman on board who had sailed with Ribault on a previous voyage. His intent to rescue the Huguenots was thwarted by the French leader of the Fort Caroline Huguenots, Rene' de Laudonniere. As it turned out, that was a fatal mistake by the Frenchman. The Spanish were successful, with the help of inclement weather, to rid Florida of the French.

In the Beginning...

The first recorded history I could find of pirates visiting St. Augustine was when Sir Francis Drake, along with 2,000 pirates, attacked the town on June 7, 1586. He ransacked the town and stole 2,000 pounds sterling and a treasure chest of military pay that was supposed to be for the Spanish soldiers who were stationed there. Also taken was some bronze artillery. When Sir Francis left, he burned the town and only the bravery of a black Spanish soldier, Juan Fernandez, and Native American allies saved some of the townspeople. They created a diversion in front of Francis Drake's men and the people escaped into the swamp area. Francis Drake was eventually knighted by the Queen of England for filling her coffers with the spoils from his pirate raids. Which just goes to show you, if you know the right people...

Robert Searles

On May 29, 1668, the English pirate Robert Searles, (alias, John Davis) came into the harbor on a Spanish supply ship captured off the coast of Cuba. In the evening, his crew disembarked and looted the town killing sixty people. The governor at that time, Francisco de la Guerra de la Vega, slipped out a side door of his home and ran to the town fort for safety. Before he left, Searles, ransomed off prisoners for supplies and captured the Indians, free blacks, Mestizo residents, and anyone who he determined was not full-blooded Spanish. He then sold them or used them as slaves.

Robert Searles did not get off "Scott free" however. The ghost of a five-year-old little girl, who was murdered by Searles during the raid, haunted him for the rest of his life. The haunting eventually drove him mad and he killed himself years later.

Andrew Ranson

Another pirate in 1684, besides Sir Francis Drake, who did well, was Andrew Ranson. He was captured and sentenced to death in a public garroting. The Spanish used this method of execution. They would put a rope around the person's neck and turn the rope, strangling the person. After six turns of the rope. During Ranson's execution, he collapsed, but the executioner decided on one more twist of the rope. The Franciscan monks chanted and the townspeople were praying for the pirate's immortal soul. While the church bells rang, the rope broke. The Franciscan monks rushed forward and rescued the unconscious man, then gave him sanctuary. They determined he was spared by "Divine Intervention."

The governor of Florida at the time of Ranson's so-called execution was unable to persuade the Franciscan monks to release Ranson. The governor eventually left Florida in 1687, after failing to have Ranson properly executed.

The next governor needed workers to help build the new fort, and the ever-opportunistic Ranson, who had engineering and carpentry skills, offered to help, if the governor would spare his life. The governor agreed. Ranson also helped to defend the fort against an attack by the South Carolina governor and his troops. After that, Ranson walked out of St. Augustine a free man. No one knows for sure what happened to Ranson once he left, but the rumor is that he eventually married the governor's daughter, and there are many thousands of his descendants.

Blackbeard

One of the more colorful pirates of that era is Blackbeard in 1718. He was born an Englishman by the name of Edward Teach. Because of his dark beard that covered most of his face, he received the nickname of Blackbeard. He stood 6'4" tall and weighed 250 lbs. When he would attack a ship with his pirate crew, he had the habit of setting his hair on fire around his face using a slow burning material that caused a most fearsome sight while he was attacking. He would carry his dagger between his teeth, and with his pistol in one hand, would come onto the ships screaming and yelling to the terrified passengers and crew. They must have thought the devil himself was coming after them.

Blackbeard met his end during a battle off the coast of North Carolina by an English Lieutenant with the Royal Navy by the name of Robert Maynard. The lieutenant finally killed Blackbeard, after a long drawn-out battle in which Blackbeard was wounded numerous times. He died only after he had been shot twenty-five times. Lieutenant Maynard cut off Blackbeard's head and hung it from the top of the English ship. The rest of Blackbeard's body was tossed overboard, and the legend is that his headless corpse swam around and around the ship looking for his head, before sinking to the bottom of the ocean.

Does Blackbeard's body still swim around in the Atlantic Ocean looking for his head? A scary thought. He could be anywhere, maybe off the coast of Florida.

The life of a Pirate was not as glamorous as the movies portray. As you can see, they were also hung by the neck, hunted, and haunted...

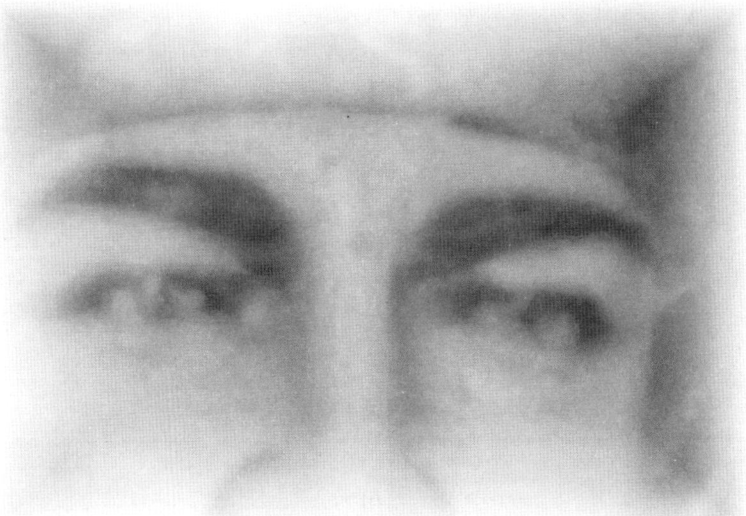

The Watchtowers

No longer there
(But a part of the history of St. Augustine!)

Out on the coastline called Matanzas Inlet, during several different time periods, watchtowers were constructed and a total of six men working in shifts were posted to watch the coastline. The towers were tall wooden structures and there was a small thatch-roofed home nearby for the watchmen to live in. Whenever they would spot a ship, one of the watchmen would run to the town, or go by small boat, to warn the people of any coming danger. By this method of warning, two more pirate attacks were fought off by soldiers.

The first pirate attack avoided, involved English pirates in March of 1683, when the townspeople were warned, the towns' soldiers and ships were able to come out and defend the town against the pirate invaders.

Another attack occurred on May 1, 1686, when French pirate Michel de Grammont tried to raid St. Augustine again by way of Matanzas Inlet. The Spanish took fifty men with them, and after a four hour combat, were able to resist the pirate invaders. The local Indians finished off any pirates that were left on land, but the pirates who had stayed on the ship sailed up the coast to form a blockade. That ended when the Spanish sent a ship to Cuba, and according to records, the Pirate Grammont was lost at sea in April of that year.

Watchtower Ghost?

The watchtowers are no longer standing, but archaeological evidence shows there were at least seven of them constructed over the years. Because they were made of wood, the elements soon destroyed what the pirates couldn't.

On a winter day on January 24, 1785, a small band of pirates, (four men), rowed to shore west of Anastasia Island to loot a house that belonged to a man named Jesse Bell. After robbing the house, they were returning to the boat and one of the pirates, Thomas Bell, fell to the ground wounded and was left behind. He was carried to the town plaza where he died and his body was shown on the gallows of the old fort the next day.

Maybe the ghost of the old pirate is the one in the watchtower of the new fort looking for his ship to return for him? But, they *were* pirates after all. Don't you know that the other raiders probably weren't concerned about him; they just wanted to save their own skin.

A Haunting Amongst Pirates

There is even a rumor there were thirteen pirates hung in the vicinity of the lighthouse on Anastasia Island. That would help explain some of the spirit activity on the Island. Some of it scary, according to a local resident on the island who bought a house with a haunted laundry room. Not a pleasant experience for her, and the house has a strong, determined spirit in it. One psychic called the area in the laundry room a "gateway to hell." Which would explain the negative energy created by any spirits who may be lurking there.

The pirates certainly would create enough negative energy for a "gateway to hell!"

37

The Spanish Military Hospital

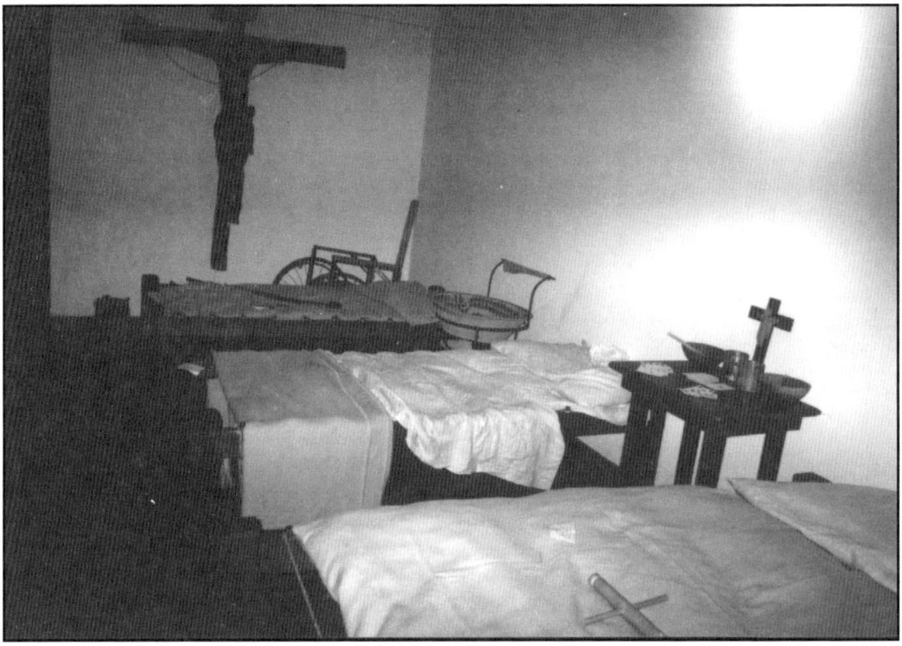

Spanish Military Hospital with Spirit Lights

3 Aviles Street
St. Augustine, Florida

Also known as The Hospital of Our Lady of Guadalupe, it is one of the more interesting haunted buildings in St. Augustine and has quite a ghostly history behind it. When I visited the building and took photos, I was greatly surprised when the pictures were developed.

There is a huge white light over the tour guide with tendrils of light coming off it. I felt a presence while I was there and was slightly uncomfortable while touring the building. The place where the white light appeared was in the room where the guide was showing me the instruments that were used, while operating on patients. I was fascinated by the story of the operations and could not imagine having to go through an amputation without anything to sedate you. The guide said the operations were performed upstairs and outside as the surgeons needed the daylight hours to be able to see what they were doing.

As St. Augustine was a very small town at the time, I'm sure the residents heard a lot of screaming and yelling coming from that area. Can you imagine how it must have been to live close to the hospital? I wonder if they warned the residents when they were getting ready to operate? Probably not; the residents were more than likely made aware of it when the doctors performed the actual surgery.

The Spaniards were somewhat ahead of themselves as far as surgery was concerned and were more modern with their ideas of cleanliness. The tour guide said their survival rate was quite high for that day and time. They believed in cleaning the instruments and kept the hospital itself quite clean. They used prisoners from the old fort as orderlies.

Women were not allowed in the hospital except in the mourning room, which is off the front entrance of the hospital. Whenever someone was getting ready to die, a large bell was rung to summon the priest to come to give the patient last rites, and that is when the women relatives were allowed in.

The hospital only had three beds in the recovery room. (Maybe they expected no more survivors at a time?) The beds were made of wood with rope strung across the bottom of the mattresses to hold up the straw mattresses the men slept on. I would guess that the comfort of those beds was more than they were used to, as soldiers, on an ordinary basis.

There is also a pharmacy attached to the area off the recovery room and people would sit and wait there to get their medication. It has a long wooden bench for the patients to sit on, not unlike pharmacies of today with people having to sit and wait for their medicine. Some things just never change.

Ghostly Activity

I was talking to a lady from Jacksonville who used to belong to a Ghost hunter's organization in the Jacksonville area. She related an incident that happened to her while she and her husband were visiting the Spanish Military Hospital. Her husband was standing just in front of her in the pharmacy area of the old hospital when he took a step forward. Just as he did that, the wooden bench she was sitting on suddenly just picked her up and dropped her down.

Spanish Military Hospital with Spirit Lights

It gave her quite a start, as I would imagine it would anyone if something like that happened to them. She asked her husband why he had stepped forward at that time and he said he had felt a cool breeze go across his legs.

The tour guide said the most spirit activity is in the recovery room area, but I found it to be around her. I felt a presence following us as we made our way through the museum. I could feel a presence in the recovery room area, but nothing showed up on the film, except a light over the bed area.

The white light around the tour guide with the tendrils of light is a form of spirit activity and shows spirit is very active in the room. I felt a spirit following us as we made the tour and it felt like a former patient. I wonder if some of the pain and suffering the patients felt is still being carried around by them and dropping someone off a bench is their way of getting even?

Fort Castillo de San Marcos

Ft. Castillo de San Marcos

1 South Castillo Drive
St. Augustine, Florida
Phone: 904-824-6506

The old fort, as we used to call it when I lived in Florida, has been around for many hundreds of years.

When I first visited the fort, it was with a group of school children, and the most outstanding thing I can remember is when they told us about Osceola, the Seminole Indian Chief who escaped from the fort. The tour guides took us into a room that had a very small window high up in the wall. How did this Indian manage to make himself small enough to squeeze through that small opening?

Not once, during the years I visited the old fort was anything mentioned about the fort itself being haunted. During my trips to St. Augustine to do the research, I discovered that, yes, there is more than one ghost haunting the old fort.

The Ghosts of the Fort

The first ghost that I heard about haunts the watchtowers. The fort is built in the shape of a square with four triangular-shaped buildings off each corner of the square, and the watchtowers are at each point of the triangle. This makes it easy for a guard to spot the enemy coming from almost any direction.

The Spanish built the fort starting in 1672 and finished twenty-three years later in 1695, using coquina shell from nearby Anastasia Island as the basis for the rock. This rock is plentiful on the Florida beaches and if you have ever walked on it, you can see how it would withstand the elements. The coquina crunches beneath your feet as you walk along a shoreline. It is easy to understand why this shell was used to construct not only the fort, but some of the houses in the area.

The first ghostly story is of a specter of a guard, in one of the watchtowers, who still smells of garlic and sweat centuries after he has died, and another tale is of a cloaked figure looking out over the bay from that same tower. I'm wondering if it's the old pirate who was hung and still looking for his shipmates to return?

A night watchman has seen a young woman in a white dress walking about the grounds of the fort, and when they check it out, no one is there. She appears to vanish into the trees or the walls around the fort.

A young Spanish soldier who was killed by a cannon ball while looking for a ring he dropped outside the walls of the old fort has been spotted. He appears to be still around the fort area looking for his ring as he is seen walking about while looking down in the same place where he was supposedly killed.

There was a Colonel Marti in charge of the fort at one time and the story goes, he caught his wife, Senora Delores Marti, having an affair with a Captain Manuela Abela, and he had them both chained to a wall in the old dungeon and built a matching coquina wall around them, sealing them in forever—or so he thought.

There were some workers doing renovations on the fort when a cannon fell through one of the floors. They found some old bones in a room that was uncovered by the hole. Some people think it is the bones of Senora Marti and her lover, Captain Abela. There have been reports of the smell of a ladies' perfume and eerie lights floating around in the dungeon area.

The Sounds and Spirits of War

It is also said that if you put your ear up to the walls of the fort, you can hear the sounds of battle with gunshots, yelling, and screaming. If energy can be trapped in the way of a spirit apparition, why not sound as energy trapped in the walls of the old fort? Sound is also a form of energy. If you have ever listened to the sound of the ocean a seashell makes, it would make sense that coquina shell could trap the battle sounds.

Since many Native Americans were imprisoned in the old fort, it is said these spirits are also haunting the fort. Some say Osceola's head has been seen floating around the fort. A Doctor Frederick Weedon attended to Osceola when he was very ill and lay dying in Charleston, South Carolina; this was at Fort Moultrie. The story is that he did the autopsy on Osceola and kept his head in a jar. When he died, he left it to his daughter. What she did with it, who knows? I certainly wouldn't want the darn thing hanging around my house, or floating about either.

From research, I have learned the Weedon family descendants do have some things that once belonged to Osceola. The Seminole Indian warrior was buried with full military honors when he died January 30, 1838. He had been considered a great warrior by the army and his fellow tribesmen.

Back to the story of Osceola's escape from the fort. If you ever get a chance to go to the haunted old fort, check out the room that Osceola supposedly escaped from. My feeling is that what really happened is some "wampum" changed hands there.

Haunted Restaurant and Pub

Scarlett O'Hara's Restaurant

Scarlett O'Hara's Restaurant

70 Hypolita Street
St. Augustine, Florida
Phone: 904-824-6535

One place that is advertised to be haunted is Scarlett O'Hara's Restaurant—with food worth the visit.

The story goes that a sea captain by the name of Mr. Colee, who built the house for his fiancée, was taking a bath upstairs when he drowned in the bathtub. In their ad for Scarlett O'Hara's, they show a bathtub cut out and used as a sofa. In reality, when you go to the restaurant there is no bathtub and the employees are reluctant to talk about any haunting.

A Room With a Bath

I asked where the bathtub was? I was then directed to the ladies bathroom in the upstairs bar and eating area. There is no bathtub. Only a small bathroom that would not have been big enough to hold a bathtub for a grown man. Although it is said that late at night you can hear the sound of water splashing and the moans of the old man as he lay dying in the bathtub.

I suppose if you want to get a sense of the place as being haunted you would have to visit after hours when the old man is taking his bath.

The upstairs area, where the old man drowned, is now known as "The Ghost Bar."

No More Tubs for Scarlett's

The downstairs bar area is said to have some spirit activity although my camera did not pick up anything while I was there and no one said anything to me while I was taking photos of the place.

A former renter of Scarlett O' Hara's, when it was used as a home, was an antique collector who had a fascination for *Gone With the Wind*, thus the name Scarlett O' Hara's. The man's wife was out of town visiting relatives, when two intruders broke in and beat and then drowned him in the bathtub—which seems to be a favorite means of death in that building.

When there, you will notice there are no more bathtubs in the old house. The wife was exonerated from the crime, but it was found out later that her husband was having an affair with a woman who bore a striking resemblance to Vivien Leigh, the woman who portrayed Scarlett O'Hara in the movie version of *Gone With the Wind*.

After the murder, his wife left the building, leaving behind her dead husband's collection of *Gone With the Wind* memorabilia. Some people believe the woman her husband was having an affair with had something to do with his murder, but the police were unable to prove anything. His mistress died two years later, by committing suicide.

Some of the staff have seen apparitions of the husband and his mistress in the restaurant. She wears a long black negligee, and both husband and mistress have been seen in the second story of the building, which is now a restaurant and bar area.

Scarlett O'Hara's Restaurant, downstairs area

No wonder the staff is reluctant to talk about it. Maybe they are afraid they will "summon up" the ghostly couple. One of the tour guides from the St. Augustine's ghost tours said she has seen them twice while they were sitting together at a table in the downstairs area of the restaurant and bar.

So if you plan to visit Scarlett O'Hara's—and you should—have a nice meal, but forego the bath…

Ann O'Malley's Irish Pub

23 Orange Street
St. Augustine, Florida
Phone: 904-825-4040

The stories of Ann O'Malley's Irish pub are based on the pub itself being built on top of some graves in the area—and what more one would expect from an Irish pub? The owner, Trish Nease, has said that a pot would suddenly fly off a stove for no good reason and pictures bolted to a wall will suddenly fall off. She says there have been other unexplained phenomena in the pub and doesn't have a good explanation about why it happens.

Charles Tingley of the St. Augustine Historical Society says there are no documented graves in the area, although the Tolomota Cemetery is close by, with the ancient Indian graves. During the yellow fever epidemic, there were quite a few people buried in unmarked graves that would now be under some of the streets in the area. The people were dying so quickly and there were so many of them, is it any wonder a few just got dumped in a hurry?

The oldest drug store, with Indian graves underneath it, is only just down the street from Ann O'Malley's Pub. The Huguenot Cemetery is nearby in the other direction. Located between two very old cemetery sites, who knows what spirits may have wandered into an old-fashioned Irish drinking pub? Just because someone has died, doesn't mean they aren't even now attracted to the drinking establishments. Some old ghost soldier from the nearby fort could even be enjoying another kind of spirit in the spirit world vicariously, trying to quench his thirst, still...

Haunted Houses of St. Augustine

49 St. George Street

There was a home that was above the Paffe Stationary store on St. George St. A nurse was taking care of an ailing patient there and she walked down a long hallway to get some warm milk for her charge. When she returned, there was shadowy figure of a man kneeling in front of the door to the sick room. He had been seen walking the hallways several times, and according to a Paffe relative, Joseph Paffe of Jacksonville, Florida, it is his Uncle Clement Paffe. The patient, his long-dead Uncle, is concerned about the great-grandmother of the Paffe family named Mary Jane Hernandez.

The nurse was frightened of the specter of a man walking the hallways, not aware of who he was or why he was there. He made many trips to her room to check on her and the ghost must have thought the sick woman was his elderly relative.

He still appears to be checking on people who are ill in that building.

The site of the Paffe family home is now the Pellicer-Peso de Burgo home that was constructed by the St. Augustine Preservation Society. I'm not sure if the ghost of the man concerned moved to the newer house, but maybe he decided the older woman patient didn't need him anymore and moved on. But then again, it's still another house in the same place. He could be roaming the house looking for a new patient to tend to.

Don Pedro Horruytiner House

The Governor's House
214 St. George Street
St. Augustine, Florida
(Private Residence)

The haunting of this house has a fascinating story to it. The house itself is quite old, dating from the first Spanish period of St.

Augustine and was the home of two Horruytiner families—two of whom served as Governors of Florida.

In 1821, a lady who lived in the house named Brigita Gomez saw two spirit ladies of the former Horruytiner family in the garden area. They were Maria Ruiz Horruytiner and Antonia de Pueyo. Brigita saw them and talked to them as she was tending her yellow roses in the garden. Mrs. Gomez gave one of the ladies some of the yellow roses that she had picked. When she told her husband, he refused to believe her when she said she had talked to these two women. The yellow roses she had given to one of the spirit ladies were found lying at the entryway to the house with no explanation of how they had gotten there.

The home is now owned by Mr. and Mrs. Fred Patterson, Jr. They were aware of the unusual stories of hauntings when they purchased the home and have tested the spirits themselves. On the day of the closing of the new house, they were standing in the entranceway and challenged the ghosts to let them know if they were there. Suddenly all the lights in the house came on. Mrs. Patterson is not afraid of the ghostly inhabitants, who share the home with them, from time to time.

She says there is a Spanish soldier who walks about the garden area in his uniform, who is still guarding their house. He has been seen walking about as he keeps his vigil. There was also the ghost of former Governor Don Pedro Benedict de Horruytiner, who made an entrance and tipped his hat with a long plume on it, to Mrs. Patterson and her grandson one day. She and her grandson fled the room when he appeared. Later, Mrs. Patterson found a photograph of a man posing as the governor for a modern-day promotional flyer and he was dressed exactly as she had seen the old governor, who appeared to them dressed like a well-to-do European gentleman from the 1600s.

Other unusual occurrences include finding missing items in unusual places. Jewelry that was missing was later found in an unusual jewelry box. Mrs. Patterson didn't even know the box existed, and a watch that was missing was later found in front of the bathroom door.

There is a pine box coffin in the attic left over from a physician, who kept it there whenever he occupied the home. It has moved about the floor on its' own, loud enough to be heard all over the house and from the outside of the building.

Is the old doctor who lived there still moving coffins around upstairs, getting them ready for a new corpse? Moving an old wooden coffin over the floor would create a lot of noise.

There also is a calico ghost cat that roams the premises.

Even with all these unusual happenings, the Pattersons seem to like living in the house with the ghosts and obviously don't feel threatened by them. It certainly could liven up a dull dinner party. If nothing else, maybe a ghost or two would make an unexpected appearance.

The Peterson/Firestone House

272 St. George Street
St. Augustine, Florida
(Private Residence)

Mr. and Mrs. Ralph Peterson talk of strange events happening in the home they purchased on St. George Street which they bought in the mid 60s. Tables rock back and forth and tip over, lights go off and on, and things disappear and reappear in strange places, just like in the Horruytiner home.

Mrs. Peterson says the former owner of the house, Helen Firestone, committed suicide in the garage area of the house. It's Mrs. Firestone who now haunts the premises. The Petersons are not bothered by her, but guests seem to have a hard time with the ghostly lady. She has a tendency to rock the beds and turn lights off and on at will. They don't usually stay very long. Then again, that would solve the problem of guests overstaying their welcome.

One former guest tells of an encounter with the ghost of Mrs. Firestone one night. She saw a woman dressed in white, standing at the foot of her bed and talked to her. The woman, who was visiting the family, was alone in the house. She placed a phone call to the owners relating the incident afterwards.

The visitor probably needed to tell someone about the ghostly presence or to connect with a live person to perhaps make sure she was still among the living. Encountering a ghost in a strange house would tend to make one a little nervous, especially if you are alone there with it!

Hope Street Apartment

Two sisters rented an apartment on Hope street and started having problems with it soon after. In an apartment that was tightly locked up, they would find books moved about and crumbs from leftover food on the table when they would get up in the morning. Sometimes, before opening the door to go in, they would hear sounds of people moving about inside the apartment and when they entered no one would be there.

One of the sisters decided to move, but the other one, not believing there was anything to the incidents, elected to stay. What convinced her that this was more than just her imagination was when she was awakened by someone opening her porch door to let her dog into the apartment. Then her bedroom door opened and she caught a glimpse of a hand closing her door just as her dog came running into the room. When she got up to check, no one was there.

Waking up to a door opening by a mysterious hand is a little creepy, especially if you are asleep in your bed. Even if it is just to let your dog in. No wonder her sister left the place. Doesn't seem as if the dog would be any protection against whatever or whomever would choose to come into the room.

Cincinnati Street House

24 Cincinnati Avenue
St. Augustine, Florida
(Private Residence)

There was an elderly lady who lived in the building on the second floor, and when she became ill, she was moved to a room on the ground floor where she stayed until she died. She must have preferred the second floor apartment though, because she still haunts that room. The neighbors have seen strange lights in the second-floor window. A man, called Mr. B., went with some friends of his while they were investigating the phenomena in the house.

Since Mr. B was a skeptic, he decided to stay downstairs. He was sitting on the bottom step of the staircase inside the house while the others were upstairs checking things out. As he sat there, he felt something move past him and brush up against his legs. Then he heard the footsteps go out the screen door and down the concrete front steps.

He asked the other people when they came down if they had seen anything? They advised no, but they did hear someone going down the stairs. I'm sure that made a believer out of Mr. B!

The house is now owned by a couple named Dickerson and they are restoring it, hopefully, the way the original owner, Fred Capo would have wanted it.

The mysterious Mr. B did not see the ghost, but he certainly felt its presence, as I'm sure others did who dared to venture into the house when it was vacant. Maybe the new owners have appeased the ghostly presence and it no longer needs to haunt the place, but then again, it may feel like home.

The Abbott Mansion

14 Joiner Street
St. Augustine, Florida

Constructed in the 1870s as a private home for the Abbott family, it is now run as an apartment building. Lucy Abbott, one of the family members, is said to haunt the mansion. She was a somewhat plump woman who dressed in old-fashioned clothing. Ms. Abbott actually died in a house down the street, but appears in this house because it is the first one she had built.

The other ghostly presence is an old man who dresses like a sea captain and is just called Captain by the tenants.

The current owners say they haven't seen any ghosts, but they experience problems keeping the clocks running in the house, and once, their dog was barking at the wall as if there was something in the corner.

Fate magazine published an article by former resident David Gray, who said tenants have left after only one night in the house because they have seen, heard, or felt something strange about the place. Mr. Gray said both he and his wife experienced numerous odd incidents and, at times, someone would knock on the door and, when they checked, no one would be there.

Mrs. Gray had the sensation of being pushed, which sent her falling down a flight of stairs. When she had to struggle against an unseen force trying to push her out a window, they moved out.

This doesn't sound much like a benevolent little old lady spirit to me. It seems more like "Arsenic and Old Lace."

The Abbott Mansion is now called Old Mansion in North City.

If you should happen to visit the place, I would be careful around the stairway and any open windows. The ghostly spirits appear to be very selective about who they allow in, and you may not be one of them.

The House of Death

8 Ardenta Street
St. Augustine, Florida
(Private Residence)

This house is haunted by the spirit of a woman who walks back and forth on the balcony and moves about the backyard wearing a long black cloak.

It is said there was the body of a young boy child buried in the backyard, who was born as the result of incest between the mother and her older son.

That would surely make someone feel guilty enough to haunt a place forever. I can't even imagine the consequences of a child born of incest, in a mostly Catholic community, in that day and time, or at any time in history.

(The Former) Kixie's Men's Store

138 St. George Street
St. Augustine, Florida
(No longer a men's store at this location)

One of the more detailed hauntings was told by Kenny Beeson, an employee of Kixie's Men's Store. Mr. Frank "Kixie" Kixmiller moved his store to the George Street address in 1946, and that is when strange things began to happen.

The weirdness became evident when Mr. Beeson noticed the scent of flowers around him everywhere he would go. No one else could smell the flowers and it was very disconcerting to him. Then he started to hear loud footsteps that sounded like someone walking on a wooden floor, but there was no wood floor. Kixie, it seems, heard the loud footsteps too, but didn't smell the flowers. The footsteps were heard out on St. George Street late at night when no one was around. Then doors in the shop would open, for no apparent reason, and Mr. Beeson said he could hear the sound of the door knob as it was turning. Old doorknobs are squeaky.

Then, one evening, Mr. Beeson had a friend of his, by the name of Preston Lay, visit the tailor shop. Mr. Beeson was busy hand sewing a collar on a suit. His friend, Mr. Lay, was watching a documentary on the television in the shop, while Mr. Beeson was finishing the collar. Suddenly, the stock room door opened by itself and they were surrounded by the very strong smell of cologne. When Mr. Lay made a comment about Beeson wearing some strong cologne, that's when Mr. Beeson told him he wasn't wearing cologne. They decided to check the stock room, but when they went into the stock room, the strong smell of the cologne wasn't there. It was simply around the two men. Then they heard the bathroom door close. At that point, they decided it was time to leave, so Mr. Beeson put up his sewing, turned the iron off, and they left.

Before leaving the building though, Mr. Beeson set up a tape recorder, with a thirty-minute tape on, inside the building He left the tape player on top of a sewing machine cabinet. Later, when he listened to the recording, you could hear the sound of the men leaving, then a short pause. That is when the spooky noises started. He could hear the sound of footsteps stomping around, and squeaky door knobs turning. There was a ship's bell in the store that could be heard ringing a couple of times in the background. When Kixie and the seamstress, Dorothy Giddens, listened to the noises on the tape, they were amazed.

Shortly after the incidents with the tape recorder, Mr. Beeson's friend, Preston Lay, died of a massive heart attack. They decided then that the bell ringing had been some type of warning of an imminent death.

The final straw for Kixie was when his homemade alarm system failed him. He'd had a bell installed in a drop ceiling, that would warn him whenever anyone came in, while he was working in the back of the shop. One day, the bell didn't ring as it should have, and when Kixie climbed up into the ceiling, he found that two wires had been cut. That's when he called Monsignor Harold F. Jordan to come perform an exorcism on the building. After that, the problems stopped except for the smell of flowers that stayed around Mr. Beeson. Once, inside a closed vehicle, the scent was so strong, that even Mrs. Beeson commented that she could smell the flowers.

Mr. Beeson seemed to be the conduit who attracted the ghost to begin with. He obviously had them attached to him wherever he went. It seems the ghost, or ghosts, enjoyed the car rides with him and Mrs. Beeson. One never knows who a ghost may be attracted to, could be your spouse or even a next door neighbor...

The St. Francis Inn

279 St. George Street
St. Augustine, Florida
Phone: 904-824-6068

The St. Francis Inn is one of the most haunted buildings in St. Augustine. It was built over an underground river that runs beneath the street. Henry Flagler had the river covered over, and running water is still an energy source that is useful for poltergeist activity. In 1791, Caspar Garcia built the structure as a private residence.

The stories of the haunted inn center around a young slave girl named Lily who roams the place. She wears a long white dress. (Do they all wear long white dresses?)

I was meditating about the white dresses the female ghosts seem to always be wearing. The answer that came to me is the white dresses are the easiest to manifest and is an easily recognized form of clothing from the spirit realm.

The story is about the nephew of Major William Hardee who bought the building in 1855, who fell in love with Lily. They would meet on the third floor and people found out about their illicit romance. Because of the social customs and circumstances of the times, he was unable to marry her.

He committed suicide either by hanging himself in the attic or jumping out of the third-floor window of the building. Both stories have been told recounting how he died. Either way, he was still dead by his own hands and is supposedly haunting the old place with Miss Lily. Rumor is that Lily was sent away because she was pregnant, and he was so devastated, that he killed himself.

Lily particularly plays around in room 3-A, where most of the people have had encounters with her. She likes to manipulate the water spigots and the lights—turning the water to a different temperature when someone is trying to set it and turning lights off and on at random.

She is a lighthearted and playful spirit and just likes to hang around the Inn. A couple of the innkeepers have seen her as a figure walking by. She has been described as a tiny woman with long dark hair.

Mrs. Boerema, an innkeeper, was in room 3-A with her college-age children when a light came on by itself, and they all heard a mournful wail. Even after they left the room and closed the door, they could still hear the sound of wailing coming from the room.

One of the employees of the inn was staying in room 3-A one night, when a tote bag she had carefully placed on a chair was suddenly turned upside down on the floor, with all the contents spilling out. She had been doing research on the Inn while staying there, and all her paperwork was in the bag.

John Kachuba from the book *The Ghosthunter* stayed in Lily's room and had a psychic medium from Jacksonville meet him there to see if they could get any information about the haunted room. The main thing is, Lily doesn't like things to be moved around or disturbed. If you make fun of her, she will pack your bags and leave them by the door which is a very clear message to anyone to just go away according to Kachuba!

A couple of people have seen Lily's lover and describe him as a somewhat small person who has on a military uniform with gold buttons on his coat and wears a tri-cornered hat of the colonial era.

If you decide to visit the St. Francis Inn and stay in Lily's room, leave things as they are, or you may find your bags packed, waiting by the door as a clear message to GET OUT while you still can!

Casablanca Inn

24 Avenida Menendez
St. Augustine, Florida
Phone: 904-829-0928

Another one of the well-documented haunted places is the Casablanca Inn. Part of the unusual spirit activities include a lantern seen on the widow's walk across the top of the building. This lantern has been seen by people staying at the Casa de La Paz Inn across the street from the Casablanca and by fishermen or boaters out in the harbor.

The beginning of the story is about a young woman who worked there as an innkeeper during the 1920s when prohibition abounded. The area was full of smugglers and rum runners. As a coastal town, it would be an ideal site for the numerous smugglers in the area. In this day and time, the smugglers are sending cocaine and marijuana ashore, but in the 1920s, it was booze.

The young lady innkeeper had a lover who was one of the smugglers (he later drowned at sea) and she used her place to help warn the smugglers when "revenoors" were around. As the innkeeper, she rented her place to the Federal agents as well as the smugglers. When the coast was clear and the smugglers could come to the Inn, she would walk across the widow's walk swinging her lantern. That way they could keep on sailing up the coast if it wasn't safe to come to the building. The Federal agents eventually figured out what the young lady was doing and why they were unable to catch any of the smugglers. Someone probably told the agents about her, as I'm sure not everyone was sympathetic to the smugglers. There were staunch abolitionists who lived in the area, too.

A night innkeeper heard footsteps walking in the room above him while he was working late one night, and when he went to check, there was no one there.

Young women in love seldom are smart about their lovers. I'm sure she was a good source of income for the smugglers as she also sold their booze at the inn. She received money for helping these rumrunners out, so maybe she wasn't so dumb after all. When she was eventually caught by the Federal Agents helping the smugglers, there is no record of what happened to her. She may have made enough money with her smuggling activities to hire a good lawyer.

The lady innkeeper who haunts the building is buried in the old Huguenot Cemetery. Although the she is long gone from the Casablanca, she may still feel as if she needs to warn people out on the water of "revnoors," or perhaps she is hoping her lover, who drowned, will see her with the lantern and find his way back to her?

44

Casa de la Paz Inn

22 Avenida Menendez
(Across from the Casablanca Inn)
St. Augustine, Florida
Phone: 904-829-2915

The Casa de la Paz began as a home to J. Duncan Puller in 1915. Mr. Puller was a prominent banker who traveled in high society in St. Augustine. He was living there during Henry Flagler's reign in the small town.

The house was converted to a Bed and Breakfast in 1986 and is now an apartment building.

When Mr. Puller and his family lived in the building, he invited a young couple who were on their honeymoon to stay with his family in his home. On the last day of their visit, the young groom decided to go fishing. Unfortunately for him, there was a sudden storm and his fishing boat capsized. The young man was drowned and his new wife was devastated. She stayed in the area for several years after the tragic boating accident, and eventually died of a broken heart, as the story goes.

These days she haunts the old home still waiting for her lost husband to return. Sometimes she can be heard knocking on the doors and asking, "Is it time to go yet?" And she has been seen walking in the hallway or at the top of the stairs with her suitcase packed and ready to go.

I can just imagine how devastated she must have been when she was just planning her life together with her new husband and then to suddenly have it all snatched away from her. Not many young women have to deal with that type of tragedy, and the ones who do, don't often get over it easily.

Casa de la Paz is the building that people who stay there say they have seen the lantern light on the widow's walk at the Casablanca Inn across the street. Maybe if one spends some time there, you can see a ghostly figure walking across the widow's walk warning the boaters of the "revnoors" in the area.

But don't let your mate go fishing if a storm is brewing or during the hurricane season, or you may end up walking the halls with the young widow waiting for his return in eternity.

The Union General's House

20 Valencia Street
St. Augustine, Florida

This house is now owned by Flagler College and is used as offices for the college. It was once home to two different Union Generals, John McAllister Schofield and Martin D. Hardin and their families. Both generals lived and died in that house. Mr. John Lyons, the Historical Researcher for Flagler College, works long hours, nights and on weekends. He heard noises several times when he was working there alone, but was been unable to check them out as he didn't have a key to the area where the noises were coming from. He said the sounds, which were coming from an area directly over his office, sounded like someone shuffling or pushing something across the floor.

On occasion, Mr. Lyons daughter, who was attending the college, used the house as a place to study. She kept getting the feeling of someone watching her more than once, and just had to get out of the building.

The noises were mostly happening during renovation of the building. It appears that the old generals were not happy about the unauthorized renovations taking place in "their" house.

The Lightner Museum

75 King Street, City Hall Complex
St. Augustine, Florida
Phone 904-824-2874

After talking to some people in the Jacksonville area, I discovered an important haunted building I had missed in the St. Augustine area. It is the Lightner Museum which was built by Henry Flagler as the Hotel Alcazar in 1887. It was constructed in the Spanish-Renaissance style. He used the same architects who built the Ponce De Leon Hotel across the street from the museum.

There was a pool area in the hotel, and during the early part of this century, ladies or girls had to wear extensive clothing to go "bathing." Sometimes, when it got wet, the clothing was quite heavy. That is what happened to one little girl who drowned in the pool area. She was unable to get out of the pool in her heavy, wet clothing.

Now it is said she haunts the area around the hotel. At times you can see her on a side street waving at you. She disappears, and is suddenly at the other end of the street waving again. Some people have seen her floating in the area above where the pool used to be.

The building was purchased in 1946 by Otto Lightner to house his extensive Victoriana collection. It is a beautiful old haunted building that has a lot of pieces from the Victorian era and probably would confuse a ghost as to what century they were actually in. Or where the pool is located...

Shipwrecks off the Coast of St. Augustine

Doing my research of shipwrecks off the coast of Florida, I realized they were too numerous to mention them all in this book. There have been thousands of shipwrecks off the coasts of the United States and countless lives and money lost. There are corporations now who are searching for some of these lost ships using sonar and deep water vessels to explore and salvage them. No longer is it the personality of a Mel Fisher or some lone treasure seeker who is looking for these lost galleons.

The reason I am including these shipwrecks is because St. Augustine has such a rich history of "lost at sea" stories. There have been frequent tales of wives and lovers still searching for their lost love ones to return from the sea, many years after they are gone.

Where do the spirits of these lost sailors go? Are they still aboard ships that are now ghostly vessels sailing our oceans, or do they just disappear in the netherworld? I have heard tales of "ghost or phantom," ships but how do they become phantom ships? Does the whole crew have to be present **to** manifest these ships? Or can a sea captain alone do this? There are many recorded instances of "ghost ships" which by definition are ships that appear as phantoms or abandoned ships with all the crew mysteriously missing, that are still sailing around in the ocean. No one knows what has happened to the crews of these ships and the mysteries are never solved.

Many ships were moored off the coast of St. Augustine in a 400-yard area in front of and south of the Fort Castillo de San Marco. There were three sand bars, and ships had to maneuver around and between them in bad weather; it had to be treacherous. It is said the sand bars around St. Augustine claimed most of the shipwrecks in the sixteenth and seventeenth centuries, second only to the treacherous reefs around the Florida Keys. If you have ever encountered a coral reef, you know how dangerous they can be, and I can just speculate how the wooden-hulled ships fared on these coral reefs. Sand bars are dangerous because they can't be seen at high tide. A ship is on top of one before anyone knows it and can't be moved because it is heavy and it sinks into the sand.

Ghosts and pirates are part of these sunken vessels. The sailing ships of old were actually very small ships made of wood and the people on board would be doomed to a wooden coffin, in a watery grave, slowly sinking into the ocean.

Fear and terror help to create a ghostly presence and, if they could all be seen, I would say there are specters aplenty still trying to escape their fate, and not end up at the bottom of the sea.

The following is a list of some of the shipwrecks off the coast of St. Augustine. I only listed some of the more interesting shipwrecks in the area.

HMS *Squirrel*

In May of 1790, Captain Peter Ward sunk the HMS *Squirrel* a "privateer sloop," which is a privately-owned ship commissioned by a government to attack and capture other ships during times of war. This ship was sunk off the coast of St. Augustine and was carrying Spanish Pieces of eight. Her crew swam ashore.

Prince George

On November 11, 1769, the *Prince George*, which was sailing from London to St. Augustine was lost while trying to maneuver into the port area. Most likely on one of the infamous sand bars.

Sally

February 22, 1773 the vessel *Sally* sailing from London to South Carolina lost all her crew, except for the first mate, in a snow storm off the coast of St. Augustine. A snow storm off the coast of Florida is rare, but it does happen. I remember one year while I was living in Nashville, Tennessee, in the 1980s, there was a bad snow storm that extended all the way from Nashville to my parents home in Jacksonville, Florida. It actually froze the canal off the St. Johns River behind their home and Mom said the seagulls in the area became disoriented and would slide on the ice when they tried to dive for fish.

Dove

On October 18, 1773, a ship called the *Dove* sank, a strange name for this ship as it was a slave ship, sailing from Africa to St.

Augustine. It was lost off the coast of Florida, killing the Slave Master, two crewmen and 80 of the 100 slaves aboard the ship.

A Schooner

In November of 1779, there was a schooner sailing from Ogeechee, Georgia, with sick and wounded Americans aboard, which was driven ashore and the people were made prisoners.

O. C. White's Seafood & Spirits

118 Avenue Menendez
St. Augustine, Florida
Phone: 904-824-0808

O. C. White's (which stands for *Out of Control*) is one of the better-known haunted restaurants in St. Augustine.

It was once the home of Mrs. William J. Worth, whose husband was a major general in the U. S. Army. He was successful in many military campaigns and is remembered with the Worth name on many cities and monuments in the country. Lake Worth, Florida, is named after him, and there is a monument dedicated to him in New York City.

One of the previous owners, (Mrs. Worth?) was a staunch abolitionist and that could explain some of the strange phenomena that happens in the building.

The original building was in the parking lot area of the current restaurant, but it was moved stone-by-stone to its present location. The home was built in 1791 by Don Miguel Yanardy, a prominent merchant ship owner and building contractor. The home changed hands and identities several times until it was bought in the mid 1800s by the widow of William J. Worth, who was also a major military figure in the Mexican-American War. Mrs. Worth and a daughter lived there until she died in 1869. Another daughter lived in the home until it was purchased in 1904 by George Potter, the once owner of Potter's Wax Museum. He then moved the house, stone-by-stone, to its present location.

Trouble Brewing

Once it was established as restaurant and a bar, the trouble started. A mysterious and very strange fire broke out in the second floor of the building on Friday the 13th, 1992. The heat was so intense, it blew out the window on the second floor and scorched an office on the third floor; although the walls and ceiling were charred, the floor did not burn through. The only thing that survived was a photograph of the original mansion as it stood in the old parking lot area. The area around it was scorched, but the painting itself, did not burn. When, Dave White, the current owner, came in to put plywood up on the windows, he heard a woman scream at him from an open area in the floor. No one was down below and the sound was coming from above the hole in the floor. He quickly packed up his work tools and left the building.

Dave, himself, has had several strange occurrences in the building. He thinks it is old Mrs. Worth. The upstairs office door has a new lock and deadbolt on it, which he locks whenever he leaves the room. No matter, whenever he puts the key in to unlock the door, before he can even turn the key, the door swings open. He even had the door completely re-hung and new locks put on it. Still the door opens before he can unlock it.

O. C. White's Seafood & Spirits Restaurant. Objects in the restaurant move around on their own.

There is a set of beads that get moved around in the restaurant. They were originally hung on a jaguar head and then on a ship's figurehead, then back to the jaguar. Mrs. Worth, or someone, likes playing with the beads.

A waitress named, Jennifer, saw dancing salt and pepper shakers on a table when she had just taken an order from a couple who were sitting at the next table. She called two more servers over and the five people, the couple at the other table and three servers, watched as the salt a pepper shakers did their dance on the table. Stopping once and starting back up again.

An employee came into work one afternoon to help set up the place before opening, and when she went upstairs to the second floor, there was a lit candle sitting on a table burning by itself. The night before, she had blown all the candles out, and the night manager had not seen any candles burning after that. When she went downstairs to tell someone else about it, she was informed that it "happened all the time."

A prep cook came in one day to start getting things ready and was using a recipe book that is organized in a ring binder; she laid the book down to go do to the restroom. When she came back, the book was on the floor with all the recipes pulled out of it—now lying all over the floor. She picked them up and put the book back together again and a half hour later, when she had to leave the room again, the recipe book was all over the floor with the pages pulled out, when she returned. She then went outside to wait for someone else to come to the restaurant. I would imagine it would be hard to keep good help with all the strange occurrences and happenings in the building.

As late as this past August, Wendy White Putney, Dave White's sister, was working in the restaurant, and while she was on the phone, she heard a loud noise. When she went to investigate, there was a metal container full of plastic cups and lids thrown all over the floor. She said the container sits securely on a shelf and could not have fallen off by itself.

It seems to me Mrs. Worth has not been able to stop the restaurant from selling the "demon rum" or make the owners leave the building, so maybe she just amuses herself by creating mischief around the place. She probably hopes to scare a few patrons away, but obviously that has not worked either.

Daytona/Deland Areas

History of Daytona and Daytona Beaches, Florida

Another area of the coastline of Florida is the Daytona and Daytona Beaches areas. These days, the Daytona Beaches area consists of Ormond, Holly Hill, Port Orange, South Daytona, Daytona Beach Shores, Ponce Inlet, and Wilbur by the Sea.

Many, many years before all this was established, the Timucuan Indians claimed the area. They were here over 4,000 years ago, and were descended from an original aborigine tribe. The first recorded history of the Daytona area began with the arrival of the Spanish explorer Juan Ponce de Leon in 1573, while he was still looking for the legendary Fountain of Youth he thought was located in the St. Augustine, Florida, area. Daytona was not colonized until 1713 however, by the British and Spanish. Numerous plantations flourished in the area but were abandoned when the turmoil of the political climate and the warring factions with the Seminole Indian tribes gained control of the area.

When the Seminole Indians were threatened with immigration from the area, they went on a rampage and burned all the homes south of St. Augustine. The second Seminole war lasted from 1835 to 1842. In 1871, after the Civil War and things had settled down, the area was a prime location for people to move to, and away from all the problems from the war. Mathias Day laid out and plotted the area to be named after him and to become Daytona, as it is known today.

The First Race

With racing as the prime attraction to Daytona, it is only fitting that we mention the first race held in Daytona which was held in 1902 on the beach itself. Two automobiles entered into the race, reaching an unheard of speed of fifty-seven miles per hour. By 1938, NASCAR was on the scene and Speed Weeks were established—the rest, as they say, "is history!"

Movies have been made about the beach with teenagers as the prime actors in the movie pictures. Who can forget America's sweetheart, Annette Funicello, and heartthrob Frankie Avalon, in the old beach blanket movies? The beach has always held a fascination for teens in the area, as it is one place you could always go without an adult hanging over your head. With the police patrols on the beach and lifeguards looking out for you, I'm sure parents felt it was safe to let their teenagers hang out at the beach. Little did they know what was really going on behind those sand dunes!

Along with the automobile, there was the railroad that ran from Jacksonville to the West Palm Beach areas. It carried the well-to-do people from up north to their winter homes in Palm Beach. Following is a ghostly story of just such a train.

The Ghost Train

A rather fascinating tale is of a steam engine train called the *U. S. Grant* that ran from Jacksonville to West Palm Beach, Florida, on a regular basis. It was in operation from the years 1892 until 1896, when more powerful locomotives came into use and retired the *U. S. Grant* to a rail yard in Jacksonville, Florida. The home of old broken down trains.

Workers these days who go out to work on the rails at night sometimes hear the long slow whistle of a train and see a bright light coming at them. They can feel the rumble of the train as it moves over the tracks, but no train ever comes by. The railroad men have decided the *U. S. Grant* should still make its rounds to West Palm Beach and back.

Lilian's Bed and Breakfast

111 Silver Beach Avenue
Daytona Beach, Florida
(Near Ponce Inlet)
Phone: 386-323-9913

There is an old Victorian bed and breakfast in the Daytona Beach area that, as the story goes, was built on top of an old Indian Mound. Built in 1884 by Lawrence Thompson, the place was named for his sister, Lilian. It was owned by the Thompson family for 101 years, and when it was sold to Suzanne and Mike Piccitiello, it was converted into a bed and breakfast inn.

Over thirty years ago, a man who was a previous owner, saw Lilian standing in one of the bedrooms wearing (what else?) a long white dress.

When the Piccitiello's came downstairs one Christmas morning and found their nine-foot Christmas tree wedged between their glass coffee table and sofa, without an ornament or light broken on it anywhere, they decided it was time to call the Ghosthunters Society and have the place checked out.

The ghost hunters definitely found a presence in the home, and while they were there, smelled roses in a room where there were no flowers. Lilian, it seems, lives in the widow's walk area and must venture down occasionally to check *her* place out. She appears as a friendly spirit and has never caused them any real trouble. She just adds a little Victorian atmosphere to the place.

The Ghosthunter Society

Many thanks go to Dusty Smith and her organization of ghost hunters in the Daytona Beaches area for the following six stories. You can contact Dusty at her web site if you want to know more about what they are doing in the research area of ghost hunting. They have many documented cases and these are only a few of them. You can access Dusty's website at www.dbprginc.org. She has other businesses affiliated with the society which are interesting to look at and you may want to check them out.

The Ghost of the Orange Avenue Bridge
Daytona Beach

Orange Ave Bridge, Daytona Beach, Florida

Daytona Beach, Florida

A ghost of a young lady wearing a long dark cloak and walking on the bridge has been seen by several people. They have even gone so far as to give her a ride across the bridge to the Orange Avenue side and then she vanishes from the back seat of the car.

There was a young lady who was raised by her grandmother who used to like to wear her grandmother's long cloak. She was on her way to a homecoming dance one evening and was walking across the bridge when she was struck and killed by a passing car. Her shoes ended up under the bridge and her cloak was laid across the railing. The people at the accident scene said it was as if someone just laid it across the railing. These days she can sometimes be a hostile ghost and will throw things at the passing cars. Sometimes it's soda bottles or cans and even chairs have been thrown at the cars. She usually starts appearing around the time of homecoming festivities.

If you should happen to see a young lady hitchhiker and pick her up, she may only want to ride to the other side of the bridge. You may want to help her across the bridge regardless—you don't want your car damaged by flying objects...

Ghosts at the Courthouse Deland, Florida

Deland, Florida

Husbands who refuse to let go of their wives are well known to also be abusive and controlling. One such husband who had a jealous and violent temper was this type of man in the following story.

There was a couple from the 1980s who were not getting along and the wife, tiring of his jealousy and tirades, decided to seek a divorce. He would not leave her alone though, and she even had to get a restraining order out against him. He spent thirty days in jail, but after his release is when the real trouble started.

Before the divorce and when they appeared in court, the judge had to cite him numerous times for his outbursts in court. Two days after he was released from jail, the final divorce hearing was brought before the judge. After reviewing the case, the judge asked both parties if they understood what the procedure was and they both agreed. The man only reluctantly nodding his head yes, instead of a verbal answer, but the judge took that as his acknowledgment. The husband just sat stone-faced throughout the whole final hearing. Not saying a word, just staring at nothing. I'm sure they could feel the animosity emanating from him in the room around them.

Once the divorce was finalized the wife's attorney asked the court bailiff to keep the husband in the courthouse until he could get the wife safely to her car. The bailiff only said he would "try." As it turned out, he didn't try hard enough.

The wife's attorney was walking her down the courthouse steps, when suddenly the doors to the courthouse burst open and the now ex-husband came running out, pulling a pistol from out of the waistband of his pants, he shot his wife's attorney two times. The wife had tried to hide behind the attorney, but only succeeded in getting him shot the second time. She then tried to leave, but the husband said to her, "If I can't have you, no one can!" and shot her in the chest. As she lay dying on the courthouse steps, he walked over and gently stroked her hair, put his wedding band back on her finger, and kissed her on the cheek, before putting the gun to his own temple. He told her again, "the vows were until death do us part and this is where we part," pulling the trigger and falling over her dead body as he died.

There have been many reports of people finding a gold wedding ring at the bottom of the stone steps, but when they try to pick it up to show someone, the ring has disappeared. In the early Spring, just before it becomes the rainy season in Florida, you can sometimes see the outlines of the bodies laying at the bottom of the steps to the courthouse. A psychic imprint of the violence of a jealous husband and his long suffering wife.

The Athens Theatre
Deland, Florida

124 North Florida Avenue
Deland, Florida
Phone: 386-738-7156

The Athens Theatre first opened its doors as a vaudeville entertainment center in January of 1922. With live stage performances, black and white silent films and a Wurlitzer pipe organ providing the music for it all. The theatre has a long history with the people of Deland, providing them with memories of first dates and so on. The early years during the depression, the theatre was filled with children who used RC cola caps and nine cents in their pockets, to enjoy the movies and be a cheap babysitter for the parents. I can even remember the days of ten-cent admissions and staying all afternoon at the movies. The theater would be full of kids, but I think we were all spellbound in those days by the movies on the big screens.

The Main Street Deland Association purchased the building in 1994 to restore it and these days the restoration is still going on, but by the Sands Theater Group. It is due to re-open sometime in 2008.

The spirits who haunt the building are restless and remain active in the building. There is one story of a stagehand who was working on the building and fell from the balcony. His tool belt caught on the balcony, and before he could be rescued, he fell and died of his injuries from the fall. These days if you stand on the balcony, you can feel it sway from the stagehand still trying to get free of his hanging tool belt before falling again.

The other story has its origins in infidelity. There was a young actress who was starring in a long-running play with the theater. The theater manager recognized her talents outside of the play and a torrid affair began between them. The affair was discovered by the man's wife when she showed up unexpectedly one day and caught her husband and the young actress with their "pants down." A screaming match between the wife and actress ensued and the young lady fled the dressing room half dressed—the wife calling the lady a harlot who led her husband astray, and the actress calling the wife a frigid cold fish. In her anger, the wife grabbed a brass lamp, and that was the end of the actress.

These days, the actress still haunts the theater and when anyone enters "her" dressing room whom she doesn't like, she lowers the temperature about twenty degrees or throws large and heavy objects at them. She can still be heard singing and laughing or moaning eerily about the different areas in the theater. The wife may have bludgeoned her to death, but she still didn't keep her out of the theater.

Pioneer Justice in Deland

The Girl in the Lake

In the early pioneer days of Deland, justice was meted out by a group of men who represented the "moral majority" of that day and time. No matter what the crime, and even if someone was innocent, it didn't mattered to them. Their brand of justice consisted of a short rope and a sturdy tree limb, from a tall oak tree in Earl Brown Park. These days, we would call them vigilantes, but in those days, they considered themselves the law.

One day, a freed African-American slave named William came into town. He established himself as a orange grove owner and made friends with the local population. Once he had his business going, he decided he needed a wife and family to make it all complete. Going to the Sunday picnic after church services, he lay on the ground when a shadow passed over his vision. Looking up, he saw a young lady who asked him about the pie he had brought to the social. Her name was Eliza. They struck up a conversation and when it was time to leave, he offered her a ride on his mule back to her home. She jumped up on the back of his mule and they headed to her house. Along the way, they passed the local saloon, and when the men hanging around outside, saw this young white girl on the back of the mule with William, they let them know how they felt about it. Giving the mule a kick, William hurried them on. When they came to her house, he left her at the end of the long dirt road that led to her home. Giving him a quick kiss on his cheek, before she jumped down, they agreed to meet again the following Sunday after church.

Late that night, as William lay in his bed going over the events of the day and what it could mean to him, he heard a strange noise in his barn. Running out to investigate, he found the men from the saloon waiting for him with a rope and a gunny sack. One man carried a club in his hand. After beating William unconscious, they slung him across the back of his mule and took him to Earl Brown Park.

The next day when Eliza went to the store to buy material to make herself a new dress to wear to meet William in the following

Sunday, she noticed a crowd down by the lake. Curious, she made her way to the front of the crowd, and saw William hanging dead from the tall oak tree by the lake. Distraught, she ran home and would not come out of her bedroom for days. The next Sunday she was at church, but kept her head bowed in prayer during the whole service. After the church service, she wandered off by herself and her family decided it was best to leave her alone, but kept an eye on her, just in case the men from the saloon decided to go after her too.

When they missed her after a little bit, they went looking for her and found her at the edge of the lake smearing mud all over herself. She then walked out into the lake and before anyone could get to her, she drowned herself. The water turned a murky muddy color where she had disappeared into the middle of the lake.

In the late summer on the south side of the lake, sometimes you can catch a glimpse of Eliza as she is walking into the lake again. The water in the middle of the lake will turn a brown murky color at the spot where, in her grief, she drowned herself many years ago.

The Mill Worker's Accident

Daytona, Florida

In the early 1900s, the sawmill was a thriving enterprise in the Daytona area. One mill worker by the name of Dan Sawyer, had worked for the lumber mill for many years as a faithful employee. One day, quite by accident, he slipped and fell into the spinning saw blades. It all happened so fast, he didn't even get a chance to cry for help. The blades quickly decapitated him and the town undertaker was called. Putting the parts of Dan Sawyer together, he took him to the morgue and prepared him for the rather large funeral that was to be held for this man who had been popular in the Daytona area.

The coffin maker who worked with him though, was a drinking man, and was not too conscientious about his work. Just making do until he could get enough money for his next drink. The old undertaker did the best he could to patch Dan up for his funeral, but not actually attaching the head back onto the body. After all, he was just getting ready to be buried; what could happen? He finally just used a high-collared shirt to cover up where Dan's head had separated from his body.

The funeral was a big deal in the town that day and his coffin was carried through town on a horse-drawn hearse. That should have spelled trouble right there. With Dan Sawyer's wife walking behind the hearse as it moved slowly through town. Suddenly, as they made a turn, the horse got spooked and reared up. When he did, the coffin containing Dan's body slid off the back, and because the coffin had not been properly nailed, it split open on the side. His body went one way and his head went the other. Mrs. Sawyer screamed and the townspeople were horrified. Beer bottles that had been used to make the satin inside the coffin appear ruffled, fell all over the road. The undertaker scrambled to put Dan back together again as best he could, but he did not put his head back exactly in the right place. All he wanted to do was get the body and Dan's head out of sight of the crowd.

Sometimes on a moonless night in the cemetery you may hear the sound of beer bottles rattling when you walk by the grave, as Dan Sawyer still tries to get his head on straight down inside the coffin.

Tickled to Death Over Her Flowers

The Pink Lady of Daytona Beach, Florida

In the Daytona area there is a story of a kind and caring lady who loved her garden and the color pink. She supposedly only wore the pink color and some say it even extended to her underwear. Her name was Katherine and her husband's name was Jonathan. He was a jealous man and watched her like a hawk, even though she never did anything to make him jealous. Unless he was jealous of her strange fascination with her flowers and the color pink. At any rate, he never trusted her.

Katherine used to love working in her garden and for many years it gave her pleasure, until as time went on, the bending and kneeling became too much for her old knees. Finally, she convinced her husband she needed help in the garden and talked him into hiring a gardener.

The husband, afraid he would have to do the work if he didn't hire someone else, reluctantly agreed. After interviewing several young men for the job, she decided on a young Latin-looking man to help her. He was good looking in an Antonia Banderas sort of way. She and her new gardener enjoyed many hours together working and taking care of her flowers. The young man who loved the garden as much as she did, spent hours talking to her about the flowers they were planting and tending to.

After a while, the husband noticed her attention to the gardener and became suspicious. He questioned the young man one day, and even though he denied any wrongdoing, was still fired on the spot.

Knowing his wife would never admit to any infidelity with the young, good-looking man, he decided to question her later. At dinner that night, he tried tricking her into admitting her affair. When the wife saw the direction the questioning was going, she became angry. When her husband, Jonathan, accused her of an indiscretion, she angrily retorted. "Not yet, but his time will come!"

In a rage, the husband reached across the table, grabbed his wife around the neck, and strangled his poor innocent wife, whose only indiscretion had been an offhand remark.

The husband then dragged her body out to the garden and decided that he would bury her in her garden, feeling that was the appropriate place for her. He dug a hole and when he filled it in, there was still a body shaped mound left. He found several trays of pink Flox flowers and covered the mound with them.

The next day the husband packed up everything he had and left town. Staying gone for seven years. When he returned, no one questioned him about where his wife was? Waiting for the new owners of his old house to leave one day, he checked the area where he had buried his wife. He then discovered she was not there anymore. It seems the young couple who had bought the house had moved her to the local cemetery, as they thought it was a family burial plot, and did not want the responsibility for the upkeep of the grave.

Distraught, he went to the Pinewood Cemetery and walked around until he found her grave with pink flowers around it. He suffered a major heart attack at the discovery, and died, falling across her grave site.

In the Spring, when the pink flowers are in bloom, you can still see the imprint of his body laying across her grave. At the house where she was murdered and buried in the garden, the people who own the house have tried to replace the pink flowers that covered her grave in the yard. No matter what they do, the pink flowers still return to the area in the garden in the shape of a female body.

Spirits in the Old Bank Building (Halifax Historical Society Museum)

Now the Halifax Historical Society Building
252 South Beach Street
Daytona Beach, Florida
Phone: 386-255-6976

The bank building was constructed in 1910 as the Merchants Bank and Financial Institution. It stayed that way until the depression and the Florida Bank and Trust was in the building from 1936 until the 1960s. The building is a two-story building with hand-painted murals on the walls and stained-glass windows. It is now used by the Halifax Historical Society as a museum depicting the many events of the area. Past and present. Native American exhibits as well as racing exhibits are featured there.

Some of the Spirit activity centered around an exhibit they had of the boardwalk area on the beach—using pewter as miniature people and buildings depicting what they perceived the area to look like in the past. At night a spirit would come in and move things around and turn parts of the exhibit over. When people who worked there came in for the morning to open the place, they never knew what they were going to find. Finally, someone *super-glued* all the miniatures to the exhibit and that put a stop to the mischief.

Another spirit that is active in the museum is a lady named Marian. She was a prominent socialite in the area and a fashion icon. Whenever she attended society functions, she always wore the latest fashions. At her wedding to a successful business man in the area, she wore an elaborate wedding gown with a long train and matching veil. When she died in 1979, her children donated her wedding gown and some of her items to the museum. It seems Marian is still attached to her things.

She has been seen about the museum by the staff and visitors to the museum. Her attachment is what is know in the spirit realm as "possessed possessions," with an attachment to things of this world.

Halifax Historical Society Museum, Daytona, Florida

At times, some of the police in the area, while walking their beat and checking things out at night, have seen her floating through the rooms in her white wedding gown.

One lady, during a function at the museum, was in the ladies restroom, when she saw a tall dark-haired woman in a long white dress reflected in the bathroom mirror. When she turned around, no one was there; when she looked in the mirror again, the woman was gone. She checked to make sure no one else was in the restroom with her, but it was only Marian in her wedding gown. Probably checking her own reflection in the mirror.

The Boot Hill Saloon

Boot Hill Saloon, Daytona, Florida

310 South Main Street
Daytona Beach, Florida
Phone: 386-258-9506

In the 1800s a building was constructed to hold three separate businesses in the one building. On the east side of the building was a cigar and barber shop, in the middle was the local saloon, and on the west end of the building was the church. These days, the pews from the church are still on that holier side of the saloon.

During the 1900s, in the Daytona areas boom time, the saloon was called the Kit Kat Club. It was a popular watering hole for the locals until the racing craze became popular in Daytona. The owners who weren't fond of racing, especially the motorcyclist, started closing down whenever they were in town, for motorcycle race week. Finally, the owners sold the tavern to one of the bartenders, Dennis MaGuire, who was more in tune with the motorcyclists and changed the name of the bar to The Boot Hill Saloon.

As the town cemetery, Pinewood, was right across the street, this was a more appropriate name for the old tavern. Once Bike Week took off, Dennis started keeping the bar open longer hours and since then it became a famous landmark in Daytona. These days, a trip to the Boot Hill is a trip into the past of bikers from all over the country. Mementos are everywhere. With the popularity of the place, the spirits are very active there, too.

The spirits who hang about the old tavern are ones who like to play with objects—doors, faucets, and pool balls. Employees say they can hear other worldly voices and footsteps when no one is there. They also feel cold spots in the rooms. One of the faucets in the ladies room will turn itself off and on. A toilet in the men's room flushes itself. The cooler door gets left open and the beer turns warm, and who want warm beer?

Pool balls roll around the tables by themselves, songs play on the jukebox when it is not plugged in and bowls of peanuts get moved around on the bar. Sometimes when the owner is there by himself, his keys will be moved to the other end of the bar. When I was down there taking photos, one of the bartenders said that just after Biketoberfest week, there is more spirit activity in the place, as the owner of the saloon died just around that time five years ago. She said things start to fall off the shelves and she figures it is just the owner making his appearance known one more time.

But as their motto goes, "Order a drink and have a seat, you're better off here than across the street!" Of course the Pinewood Cemetery *is* just across the street. Maybe the spirits who haunt the place have taken the slogan seriously?

Tombstone Silverworks

Tombstone Silverworks, Daytona, Florida

Next to Pinewood Cemetery at Main & Fairview
Daytona Beach, Florida
Phone: 386-255-3022

A chance meeting gave me information about a ghost named "Tappy." The Tombstone Silverworks is next door to the Pinewood Cemetery and used to be the funeral home for the cemetery. The funeral director made his coffins in the upstairs rooms and had to carry them downstairs for the burials next door. He is called Tappy because they can sometimes hear a tapping noise in the building similar to when he was nailing the coffins together. There is a door in the upstairs kitchen area that slams shut even with the doorstop on it.

The lady who works in the jewelry shop told me that lately she has been coming in and finding a statue of the Mayan Sun god turned around in the display case on the wall. It is a large glass case that is attached to the wall along the side of the room in the museum. The sun god sits on the top shelf on the end and is locked at night. She asked the owner if he has been moving it and he said he doesn't touch the display case; that is her area.

It has been written that the end of the Mayan calendar is coming up in our decade. Supposedly, it only goes through the year 2012 and no one knows what is going to happen after that? Maybe there is a connection there with the Mayan sun god statue. Tappy could be trying to tell her something...

Ponce Inlet Lighthouse

Ponce Inlet Lighthouse, Ponce Inlet, Florida

4931 South Peninsula Drive
Ponce Inlet, Florida
Phone: 386-761-1821

As the tallest lighthouse in Florida, Ponce Inlet lighthouse is an impressive sight at the end of Ponce Inlet. It is a huge brick-colored structure that stands out even during cloudy days. The lighthouse has 203 steps to the top and a view of the Halifax River and the Florida coastline from Daytona Beach to New Smyrna Beach, Florida.

The first lighthouse constructed on the peninsula was in 1835, but the lack of oil for the lamps and the weather doomed the lighthouse to the ocean. William H. Williams, the first lighthouse keeper, left the area after Seminole Indians attacked the lighthouse and set it on fire. Not for another fifty years was another lighthouse constructed and that is the one still standing today. The light can be seen for twenty miles away and is a working lighthouse. The new lighthouse was completed in 1887 despite the fact it was rattled by the Charleston earthquake of 1886.

An Investigation

The Daytona Beach Paranormal Research Group investigated the lighthouse and has determined there are many abnormal activities in the area. The consensus seems to be that the former first assistant lighthouse keeper, Joseph B. Davis, may be haunting the lighthouse. It seems he suffered a fatal heart attack at the top of the stairs leading to the top of the structure. When the light did not come on one day in October of 1919, Ben Stone, the second assistant keeper, climbed the stairs to check on Mr. Davis. He found him dead on the stairs. These days, at 5:30 PM, you can feel a cool breeze pass through the area, and the paint on the stairs where Davis was found won't hold its color. That area fades faster than the rest of the staircase. Also, the DBPRG investigators filmed a residual haunting of a light keeper who passes through the gate near the oil house on a regular basis. Seems he is still tending to his rounds.

Other Ghostly Resources

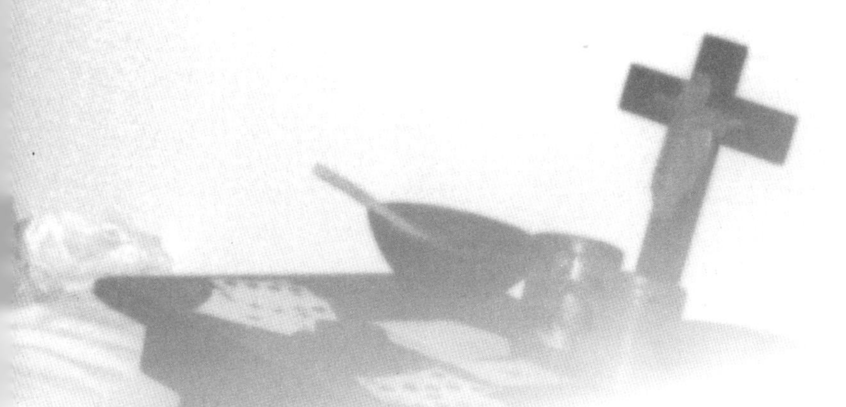

Light Orb Energy

Michael Lightweaver of the Mountain Light Sanctuary
Asheville, North Carolina
Phone: 828-626-3966
Web Site: www.mtnlightsanctuary.com

Everyone has an idea about the orbs of light that show up in photographs and almost everyone has a different idea of what they are. I first met Michael Lightweaver when I lived in Nashville, Tennessee and he ran the highly successful psychic fairs in that area. Michael is a very spiritual man and he started a retreat in the Blue Ridge mountains. He has an interesting take on the Light Orb Energy. He took an old run down area and transformed it into a place that people can go to, and get away from it all. As a very spiritually evolved person, Michael had some good ideas about how to make the place into a creative environment for people to come to and find peace and quiet. He never dreamed he would have as much light energy spread about the sanctuary that he has now.

Originally it was just one light orb taken by a camera near a stream where he had some ceramic gnomes and a pagoda that he brought back from a trip to Bali one year. Then the more he did to clear the place, and make it into a spiritual retreat, the more the light energy started manifesting. He now has fairie and elf energy and lots of Light Orbs about the place. At first he was puzzled about it all, but took it philosophically. Being a Light Worker himself, he is used to unusual occurrences, so he has learned to go with the flow. He feels the energy around his place is fairie and elf or gnome energy and I tend to agree with him.

My feeling is that orb energy is spirit energy manifesting here on earth, just to let us know we are not alone in all this. Orbs can be any energy source and there is no one on earth who can predict where they will appear. As an energy source all their own, they have *their* allegiance **in** the spirit world. In the case of the Mountain Light Sanctuary, the peaceful atmosphere and the beauty Michael is creating, probably draws them to the area—wanting to enjoy the sanctuary as it was meant to be.

Ten Recommended Florida Ghost Hunting Sites

1. If I were going ghost hunting again in Florida, I would start with the **Daytona Beach Paranormal Research Group** and contact Dusty Smith. She is one of the most knowledgeable people in that area as far as ghost research goes. She has spent many years and written several books on the subject of Daytona's haunted sites. She can be reached at: www.dbprginc.com

2. The ghost tours of St. Augustine are numerous and you can pretty much take your pick of places to go, or who to go with. The one I took was the **Ghost Hearse Rides** (123 S. George Street, phone: 904-824-8840)—it was January when I was there and it gets cold at night in Florida in January! There are also the following ghost tours:

Ghosts & Gravestones, booth in front of #2 St. George Street, St Augustine, Florida, phone: 904-826-3663

The Haunted Pub Tour, 123 St. George Street, St. Augustine, Florida, phone: 904-824-8840

Ancient City Tours—A Ghostly Encounter, 31 Orange Street, St. Augustine, Florida, phone: 904-827-0807

The Sheriff's Ghostwalk, 18 St. George Street (across from the Old Water Wheel and The Milltop Tavern), St. Augustine, Florida, phone: 904-687-9280

3. **The Athens Theater** at 124 N. Florida Avenue, Deland, Florida, would be a place I would visit not only because Deland is a beautiful small town, but also because the theater would be worth going to see. Not only for the ghostly spirits that may haunt the building, but because so much time and money has been spent to restore it to the original way it looked in the 1920s. The opening of the restored theater was scheduled for September 19, 2008 to coincide with a ten-day festival in Deland. The historic downtown area has

been restored and there are numerous restaurants nearby. The "official" grand opening of the theater, scheduled for January 6, 2009, includes celebrities and all the hoopla associated with a theater opening.

I talked to Tracy McCoy, the administrative director, and she said a ghost hunting film crew had been to the theater to film a segment there one night, but she didn't know what they had determined, so keep your eye out for a documentary with that film sequence.

4. **The Florida House Inn** at 20-22 South 3rd Street, Amelia Island, Florida (Fernandina Beach). The reason I would recommend this hotel is because it seems to be a gathering place for spirits—mostly because it feels like a "welcome station" to the ghosts. The Florida House Inn is also a great place to soak up some atmosphere. There is a history of the rich and famous from long ago staying there and just maybe one or two of them may decide to take a trip into the past and re-visit the old hotel while you are there.

5. **The Palace Saloon** at 117 Centre Street, Fernandina Beach, Florida, is like visiting a history lesson of old saloons. Especially an upscale saloon. It was designed by Adolphus Busch, the founder of the Anheuser-Busch Brewery in 1903. The original owner used to send the Rockefellers and Carnegies a monthly bill when they visited his tavern, rather than make them pay each time they ran a tab. It seems the really rich seldom carry any money with them. The Florida House Inn is within walking distance of the tavern, so I'm sure it was a popular watering hole for the very wealthy, who stayed in the area. There are stories of a former bartender who hung himself in the back bar, who still haunts the bar, and maybe you will see him still pouring a brew or two.

6. **Amelia Island Museum of History** at 233 South Third Street, Fernandina Beach, Florida. Not only does the Museum have its own history of being haunted, as the site the old jail, but it also has the Ghost Tour that is affiliated with the museum. With all the old buildings and pirate activity in the area, there is a lot to see. Not to mention the beaches that are close by.

7. **The Homestead Restaurant** at 1712 Beach Boulevard, Jacksonville Beach, Florida. The Homestead still has hauntings going on to this day. Old Mrs. Paynter, the original owner, who some say is buried out behind the restaurant, still stops by to check on the patrons. She has been seen sitting next to people on occasion. Just maybe she will visit you at your table, or you might catch her on a night when she is standing near the fireplace.

8. **The Huguenot Cemetery** at 10 South Castillo Drive, St. Augustine, Florida. I am including this cemetery over others because of the many documented ghostly encounters and the orb activity in the cemetery. Ghost hunters in Florida especially like to visit this cemetery at night. That seems to be when most of the orbs are photographed. (Please respect cemetery hours.)

9. **The Spanish Military Hospital** at 3 Aviles Street, St. Augustine, Florida. There are a lot of documented episodes of this old hospital being haunted. It could be because it was used for many years as a hospital and has a long history of pain and terror associated with it. Remember, no anesthetic was used for surgical removal of limbs. Now That is a terrifying thought by itself. Yikes!!

10. **O. C. White's Seafood & Spirits** at 118 Avenida Menendez, St. Augustine, Florida, is the final place I would recommend on a ghost hunting expedition to Florida. Mainly because it seems Old Mrs. Worth is still actively trying to scare the patrons. You just might see a dancing salt and pepper shaker on your table while you are waiting for your food.

Conclusion

After making four trips around the First Coast area of Florida researching ghost stories, pirates, and shipwrecks, I found Florida to be a more interesting place then I remembered it to be when I was growing up. I would invite people to come to the sunshine state to hunt for ghosts or just visit plain wonderful folks who still reside there. The ghostly population, on the whole, is a friendly lot and you know that "Southern Hospitality" at least, is still alive!

Selected Bibliography and Web Site Resource List

Amelia Island, Florida. www.aboutAmelia.com.

Amelia Museum. www.ameliamuseum.org.

Atlantic Theatre & Comedy Club. www.atlantictheatres.com.

Doris "Dusty" Smith Daytona Beach Paranormal Research Group. www.dbprginc.org.

Fort Clinch State Park. www.floridastateparks.org/fortclinch.

Graham, Thomas. Flagler's Magnificent Hotel. Revised edition 1990. St. Augustine Historical Society.

History of Jacksonville, Florida. www.coj.net/aboutJacksonville.

Kachuba, John. The Ghosthunter. Professor at Ohio University Dept. of English. www.johnkachuba.com.

Karen Harvey, St. Augustine Compass —Series on ghosts.

McCarthy, Kevin. Twenty Pirates. Pineapple Press, Sarasota, FL, 1994.

Michael Lightweaver. Mountain Light Sanctuary Asheville, North Carolina. www.mtnlightsanctuary.com.

Powell, Nancy and Jim Mast. Athalia Ponsell Lindsley - Bloody Sunset in St Augustine. Self published, 1998.

Professor of History The University of North Florida.

Schafer, Daniel. Anna Kinglsey. Published by St. Augustine Historical Society, 1997.

South Carolina Gazette. Shipwrecks. Lloyds of London.

The Atlantic Paranormal Society - T.A.P.S. 3297 Post Road, Warwick, RI 02886.

The Florida House Inn. www.floridahouseinn.com.

Wikipedia. www.en.wikipedia.org/wiki/Marjorie Kinnan Rawlings. Ghost Ships.

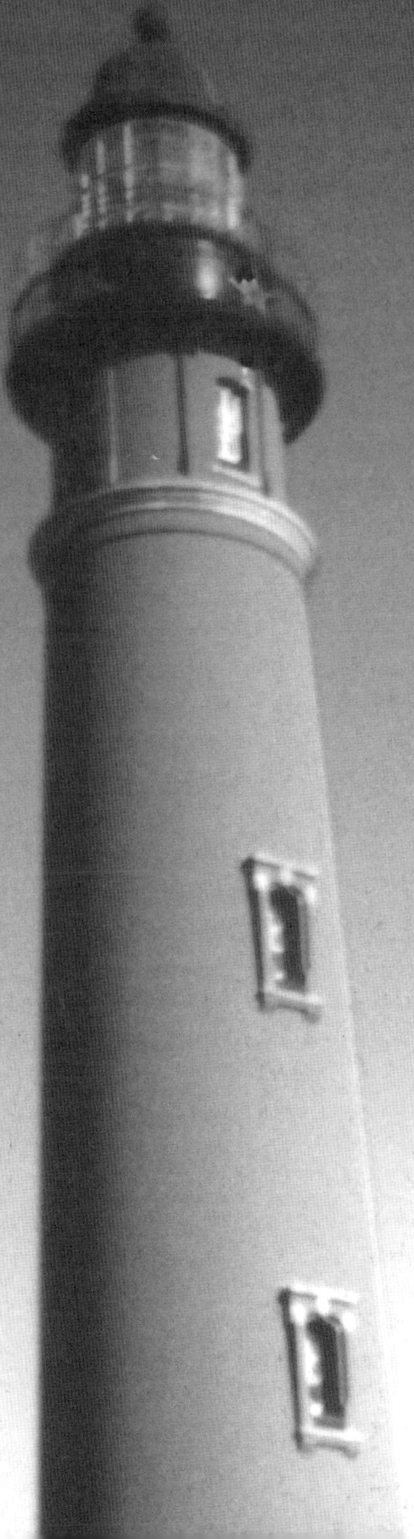

Florida Ghosts and Pirates

Jacksonville Fernandina Amelia Island St. Augustine Daytona

C. Lee Martin

Schiffer® Publishing Ltd

4880 Lower Valley Road, Atglen, Pennsylvania 19310

Library of Congress Control Number: 2008928723

Designed by Stephanie Daugherty

Type set in Artistik/ NewBskvll BT

ISBN: 978-0-7643-3020-9

Printed in China

Schiffer Books are available at special discounts for bulk purchases for sales promotions or premiums. Special editions, including personalized covers, corporate imprints, and excerpts can be created in large quantities for special needs. For more information contact the publisher:

Published by Schiffer Publishing Ltd.
4880 Lower Valley Road
Atglen, PA 19310
Phone: (610) 593-1777
Fax: (610) 593-2002
E-mail: Info@schifferbooks.com

Please visit our web site catalog at **www.schifferbooks.com.**

We are always looking for people to write books on new and related subjects. If you have an idea for a book, please contact us at the above address.

This book may be purchased from the publisher.
Include $5.00 for shipping.
Please try your bookstore first.
You may write for a free catalog.

In Europe, Schiffer books are distributed by:
Bushwood Books
6 Marksbury Ave.
Kew Gardens
Surrey TW9 4JF
England
Phone: 44 (0)208 392-8585
Fax: 44 (0)208 392-9876
E-mail:
Info@bushwoodbooks.co.uk

Website:
www.bushwoodbooks.co.uk
Free postage in the UK.
Europe: air mail at cost.
Try your bookstore first.